1000 FACTS ON
FOSSILS

Editorial Director: Belinda Gallagher
Art Director: Jo Brewer
Assistant Editor: Lucy Dowling
Editorial Assistant: Carly Blake
Designer: Candice Bekir
Picture Researcher: Laura Faulder
Indexer: Jane Parker
Production Manager: Elizabeth Brunwin
Reprographics: Anthony Cambray, Ian Paulyn
Editions Manager: Bethan Ellish

All images from the Miles Kelly Archives

Sandy Creek
122 Fifth Avenue
New York, NY 10011

www.mileskelly.net
info@mileskelly.net

www.factsforprojects.com
The one-stop homework helper

ISBN-13: 978-1-4351-0220-0

Printed and bound in China

2 4 6 8 10 9 7 5 3

1000 FACTS ON
FOSSILS

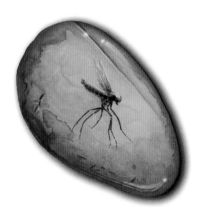

Chris and Helen Pellant

Consultant: Steve Parker

Sandy Creek

Contents

Contents

GRAPTOLITES AND ARTHROPODS

MOLLUSKS

VERTEBRATES

DINOSAURS

MAMMALS

What are fossils?

▲ *The internal chambers of this ammonite shell have filled with crystals of calcite during fossilization.*

- **Fossils** are the remains of, or evidence for, past life preserved in the rocks of the Earth's crust.

- **For the remains** of an organism to be preserved, it has to be made of material that is stable in the sediment (mud and sand) in which it is buried.

- **Usually shells**, bones, plant stems, and other remains are changed into minerals, such as calcite and quartz, for them to be preserved.

- **Creatures and plants** with hard parts are more easily preserved, as they are not easily broken before they are buried in sediment.

- **Some fossils** are simply the impressions of a shell or other organism on a rock surface. All the solid parts of the creature have disappeared.

- **Most fossils** are of organisms that lived in the sea, because here most sediment is deposited.

- **Sometimes**, whole organisms are preserved almost unaltered, such as insects trapped in amber, or mammals preserved in frozen ground.

- **Only the tiniest** fraction of creatures and plants that have lived are preserved in the "fossil record."

- **Scientists** who study fossils are called paleontologists and the science is called paleontology.

▶ *This delicate insect has been preserved complete, encased in amber.*

...FASCINATING FACT...
Some of the most delicate organic remains that have been fossilized include the feathers of primitive birds, the wings of dragonflies, and the leaves of plants.

Fossils and time

- **Paleontologists** are able to use fossils to work out many details about the Earth in the past, including how old strata (rock layers) are.

- **The sediments** in which fossils are preserved were deposited in layers, with the older layers below younger ones.

- **Certain strata** are characterized by particular fossils, and these rocks can be correlated from place to place by using their fossils.

- **Fossils** that are widespread geographically are best for this linking of strata from one area to another.

- **Fossils from the Jurassic Period** found in Britain, Europe, the Himalayas, and South America tell us that rocks in these now distant regions formed at exactly the same time.

- **Fossilized species** that only existed for a short time will only be found in a relatively thin layer of rock, and so will allow accurate correlation.

- **Ammonites and graptolites** are excellent for the relative dating of rocks.

◄ *This large ammonite, fossilized in limestone, has been eroded to reveal the suture lines.*

- **The relative geological time scale** has been established by using fossils and other geological principles.
- **Radiometric dating** is used to give absolute dates to the various parts of the time scale.
- **The time represented** by a given fossil species is called a zone, and may be as brief as 750,000 years.

▼ *This time chart shows how geological time has been divided by geologists. The absolute dates (the numbers) have been worked out using radiometric dating methods.*

ERA	PERIOD	EPOCH	AGE (MYA)
CENOZOIC	Neogene	Holocene (Recent)	From 0.01
		Pleistocene	1.8–0.01
		Pliocene	5.3–1.8
		Miocene	23–5.3
	Paleogene	Oligocene	34–23
		Eocene	56–34
		Paleocene	65–56
MESOZOIC	Cretaceous		142–65
	Jurassic		206–142
	Triassic		248–206
PALEOZOIC	Permian		290–248
	Carboniferous		354–290
	Devonian		417–354
	Silurian		443–417
	Ordovician		495–443
	Cambrian		545–495
PRECAMBRIAN TIME			4,500–545

Collecting fossils

- **Some of the most famous** and important fossils have been found by chance, but it is wise to make plans before you go collecting.

- **Fossils occur** mainly in sedimentary rocks, so there is no point looking in areas where granite or other igneous rocks occur.

- **Sedimentary rocks** such as limestone, mudstone, sandstone, and shale are formed in layers, usually on the seabed.

- **Road cuttings**, stream valleys, and seashores are good places to look for fossils, as here strata are exposed and can be easily seen.

- **A geological map** is useful to find out where sedimentary rocks, which may contain fossils, occur, but a map may not show exactly where the rocks are exposed. Strata are often obscured by buildings and roads, soil, plants and trees, and glacial debris.

- **Rocky coasts** are very good places to find fossils, as here rocks are constantly being eroded. Cliff falls bring fossil-bearing rock down to beach level. However, they should be approached with caution. Many geologists have been injured, and some killed, by rock falls from cliffs.

- **Permission** must always be sought before going onto private land, and you should never go alone.

- **A geological hammer** is useful for breaking up rocks containing fossils. Do not use an ordinary woodwork hammer, as the metal it is made of is very soft.

- **There is often no need** to quarry away at strata. Fossils are readily obtained from fallen and eroded rocks.

- **All fossils** are of scientific importance. Always wrap any specimens carefully, and record in a notebook where and when you found them.

▲ Fossils have to be carefully removed. Here, dinosaur bones are encased in plaster before they are carried away.

Naming and caring for fossils

- **Fossils are biological material**, and they are named according to the principles of biology.

- **This system**, still used today, was established in the 18th century by Carolus Linnaeus, a Swedish naturalist. Because there was a different name for each plant and animal in each language, he used mainly Latin names.

- **An organism** is generally given two names. The first is its generic name and the second its specific name.

- **The ammonite** *Hildoceras bifrons* belongs to the genus *Hildoceras*. This contains a number of species, of which *bifrons* is one. Note that biological names are written in italics.

- **These Latin words** have significance and meaning. *Hildoceras*, for example, is named after St Hilda, whose Abbey is at Whitby in North Yorkshire. This ammonite is common in strata there. The species name *"bifrons"* describes the two "brows" or ridges running around the edge of the fossil.

- **To name fossils** that you have found, it will usually be necessary to compare them with those shown in one of the many illustrated paleontology books or Internet sites.

- **Expert help** will be available at a local museum or university if you are unable to work out the name for a certain fossil.

- **Your fossils** will have to be cleaned, and any excess rock or dirt carefully removed.

◀ *These fossil mollusks have been placed in card trays, with labels to stop them rubbing against one another.*

● **It is best** to keep each fossil in a small card tray, so that there is no chance of them rubbing together.

● **The details of each fossil**, taken from your notebook, can be written on a card beneath the specimen. A number of these trays can be kept in a single drawer.

15

Extinction

- **When a species dies out**, for whatever reason, it is said to be extinct. Similar species may continue to survive, but that unique species has gone forever.

- **The fossil record** contains many breaks. A series of fossils that can be traced from layer to layer may suddenly come to an end, showing that those creatures became extinct.

- **Extinction** of one group of organisms can allow another to develop and flourish, so extinction allows the evolution of other species to take place.

- **There are countless** examples of extinction to be found when fossils are studied, from the dinosaurs to small mollusks.

- **The causes of extinction** are varied, but environmental changes can cause the death of many unrelated species, as may have happened at the end of the Permian Period, 248 million years ago.

- **A classic case** of extinction, which has been studied in detail, is that of the dinosaurs at the end of the Cretaceous Period, 65 million years ago.

- **There is considerable evidence** for a widespread change in climate and sea levels at the end of the Cretaceous Period.

- **Evidence** from various places shows that a large meteorite may have hit the Earth at about this time.

● **Dust from this meteorite impact** would obscure the sunlight and kill plants. Food chains would then be destroyed, causing widespread extinction of many different animals.

...FASCINATING FACT...
When the dinosaurs became extinct, so did 75 percent of marine plankton and very successful creatures, such as the marine ammonites.

◄ *Ammonite fossils. Ammonites became extinct at the end of the Cretaceous Period, 65 million years ago.*

17

Evolution

- **Evidence** for the development of life into its various forms can be found in the record of fossils. This change from one living thing to another is called evolution.

- **By looking at fossils**, it can clearly be seen that the more primitive plants and animals are found in the oldest rocks. However, the trilobites, which occured as long ago as the Cambrian Period (545–495 million years ago), were very well-developed creatures.

- **Evolution** is not always a steady process. It has many sudden jumps when organisms develop rapidly.

▼ *Trilobites appeared at the beginning of the Cambrian Period. They probably evolved from soft-bodied Precambrian creatures.*

- **During the Precambrian Era** (before 545 million years ago) life was probably very primitive, but for various reasons the fossil record from this time is extremely sparse.

- **At the start** of the Cambrian Period a rapid explosion of life forms occured. Trilobites and many other invertebrates were suddenly numerous.

- **In the Jurassic Period** (206–142 million years ago) sea urchins suddenly developed and evolved.

◄ *Charles Darwin was one of the first scientists to publish a theory of evolution of organisms.*

- **Charles Darwin's** famous book on evolution *The Origin of the Species*, was published in 1859. His theories of natural selection and the survival of the organisms best suited to a certain habitat are still accepted by most scientists today.

- **Modern scientists** are trying to increase our knowledge of evolution. Darwin didn't have access to new scientific ideas about DNA and genetics.

- **Mutation** is one of the keys to evolution. It is a change in the DNA of an organism, which may occur because of chemical or environmental influence.

- **Humans have influenced** the evolution of various organisms. Where industrial pollution has produced dark, grimy tree trunks, a dark form of the peppered moth has evolved, which is camouflaged in this habitat. Human misuse of the environment has driven many species to extinction.

Tracks, trails, and burrows

- **Sedimentary rocks** can be formed as layers on the seabed, the land surface, a lake, or river bed. These layers (strata) were at one time the Earth's surface, and they often have puzzling grooves and trails running over them.

- **Along with a wide range** of other structures, these trails are called trace fossils.

- **A fossil**, the record of past life, does not have to be a shell, bone, or leaf. It can be a burrow, track, eggshell, or dropping that tells us that a creature or plant has existed.

- **The study of** these trace fossils is called ichnology.

- **Trace fossils** are given scientific names, like other fossils.

- **Some of the most famous** trace fossils are dinosaur footprints. These can be used to work out the size and speed of a dinosaur.

▲ *These narrow grooves were probably made by mollusks moving over wet mud on the Carboniferous seabed.*

- **For a trace fossil**, such as a burrow or arthropod track, to be preserved, it must be filled in with mud or sand very soon after it is made, or it will be washed away.

- **In some cases**, the fossil of the mollusk or shrimp that has made a trace fossil is found at the end of its fossil burrow.

- **Dinosaur eggs** are trace fossils. Nests of *Protoceratops'* eggs and young have been found in Mongolia.

- **A trace fossil** called *Cruziana* occurs in many strata of Paleozoic and Mesozoic age. Originally, it was thought to be the trail of a trilobite, but these arthropods became extinct in the late Paleozoic. It is possible that a number of different arthropods made very similar trails.

▶ *Dinosaurs, like this* Protoceratops, *scraped nests in the ground to lay their eggs in.*

Rocks made of fossils

- **Some sedimentary rocks** are made almost entirely of fossils and fossil fragments.

- **Coal**, which has been one of the most important fuels since the 1800s, is made of the altered fossil remains of plants.

- **The finest fossils** are usually found in rocks that are made of very small particles of sediment. These are able to preserve details. Also, such sediment is less likely to crush the original organism as it is buried.

- **There are a number** of types of limestone that are classified as organic limestone, meaning that they are largely made of fossil remains.

- **Crinoids** are marine organisms related to starfish and sea urchins. They are made of calcite, and have a long, brittle stem that raises the animal off the seabed. Their broken remains, stuck together with lime mud, make crinoidal limestone—common in the Carboniferous system.

- **Chalk** is a very fine-grained, almost dusty, limestone, mainly formed during the Cretaceous Period, 142–65 million years ago. It is made of countless minute fossils, including coccoliths.

- **Coral reefs**, not unlike those that occur today, have existed at many times during the past. These reefs, rich in brachiopods, trilobites, mollusks, and corals, are sometimes preserved as fossil-rich limestone.

- **Shelly limestone** is a term used by geologists for a rock composed mainly of fossil shells. These may be of mollusks or brachiopods (lampshells).

- **Shelly limestones** may once have been banks of shells washed together by sea currents.

- **Even when** there seems to be no fossils in a rock, it may still be made largely of fossil fragments. The use of a x10 hand lens will show this.

◀ *The chalk in this cliff is almost entirely composed of fossil material, mainly tiny sea organisms called coccoliths.*

Microfossils

- **Microfossils** are tiny fossils that can only be studied with the help of a microscope. There is no actual agreed size below which a fossil is considered a microfossil. When seen at high magnification, microfossils reveal a remarkable array of shapes and structures.

- **The larger fossils**, such as shells, bones, teeth, and plant remains, are called macrofossils.

- **Microfossils are widespread** and commonly overlooked. Most sedimentary rocks contain microfossils, and a study of these can give important details about the age and environment in which the rock was formed.

- **Many microfossils** are of single-celled organisms, and the use of an electron microscope is necessary to study them.

- **The study** of fossil pollen, palynology, is a branch of micropaleontology. Pollen is a very good indicator of past climates.

- **The pure-white** limestone called chalk is made up of microfossils including coccoliths. These are single-celled, planktonic organisms with a circular structure. They are most numerous in warm seawater.

- **At certain points** in the geological record there are rocks referred to as cherts. These are silica-rich sediments, some of which are formed by accumulations of microfossils called *Radiolaria*.

- **Conodonts** are minute, toothlike fossils. Exactly what they are has been a matter of discussion. Studies of complete conodont fossils suggest that it may have been an eellike creature. They only occur in rocks from the Cambrian to Triassic ages.

▲ *Among the most common fossils are minute microfossils. These diatoms (minute, single-celled algae) are magnified many hundreds of times.*

- **Foraminifera** are single-celled organisms that live as plankton or on the seabed. Their tiny shells make up much of the "ooze" that covers the deep ocean floor.

- **Nummulites** are slightly larger types of Foraminifera that often make up nummulitic limestone. This rock was used a lot as a building stone in ancient Egypt.

The oldest fossils

- **The record of fossils** from Precambrian times (4,600–545 million years ago) is remarkably sparse. This is most of geological time, and yet we know very little about what was alive then.

- **Precambrian rocks** are often changed by metamorphism, and so any fossils they may have contained could have been removed.

- **Primitive life forms** would have had soft bodies, probably without shells, so may not have been preserved as fossils.

- **In its early years**, the Earth's atmosphere lacked oxygen and may have been composed of gases, such as water vapor, methane, and ammonia. These are not useful to life as we know it today.

◀ *During the end of the Precambrian Period many organisms developed, including these fronds of* Charnia, *probably a sea pen.*

- **Life probably** first developed around 3,500 million years ago, though there is very little fossil evidence from this time.

- **Among the earliest** fossils are 3,500 million-year-old algal remains found in Western Australia.

- **In the silica-rich** chert near Lake Superior, fossil microscopic plant cells occur, suggesting that there was more oxygen there.

- **Late in the Precambrian**, organisms became more numerous. One of the most famous groups of fossils, the "Ediacaran assemblage," comes from a number of sites, including Australia, England, Newfoundland, Scandinavia, Russia, and Africa.

- **Ediacaran fossils** include delicate organisms, such as jellyfish, worms, frondlike organisms, and sea pens.

- *Charnia* is a famous Ediacaran fossil found in 1957 in Leicestershire, UK, by a schoolboy.

Fossil algae

- **Although they are very delicate organisms**, certain algae build calcium carbonate structures that are easily preserved as fossils.

- **The best-known fossil** algal structures are called stromatolites, made by blue-green algae.

- **Algae and bacteria** work together to build the rounded mounds of layered calcium carbonate.

- **When seen in a rock face**, stromatolites are mounds of calcite. On a flat surface they look like concentrically banded disks.

- **The earliest stromatolites** are found in rocks over 3,000 million years old.

- **In the 1950s**, living stromatolite-building algae were found in Western Australia. Here, they exist in water that is highly saline, where other organisms can't survive.

- **Much Precambrian** limestone is the result of stromatolite formation.

- **Blue-green algae** produce oxygen. This vital gas began to accumulate in the Earth's early atmosphere, allowing evolution to develop oxygen-dependent organisms.

- **This abundance of oxygen** led to the formation of the ozone layer high in the atmosphere, which protects us from harmful ultraviolet radiation.

- **Stromatolites** have occurred on Earth for thousands of millions of years.

◀ *Stromatolites, such as these, are found fossilized in rocks 3,000 million years old. Similar organisms live today in Australia.*

Primitive plants

- **The first vascular plants** (plants with veins) evolved in the late Paleozoic Era.

- **In Devonian rocks** there is evidence of a rapid evolution of plants, and the Earth's surface began to look green for the first time.

- *Cooksonia* is a very early veined plant and occurred in rocks of late Silurian and Devonian age. During this period there were large landmasses on which vegetation could develop.

- **With a stiff stem**, *Cooksonia* could stand up above the surface, in which it was held by primitive roots.

- **Like modern plants**, *Cooksonia* had xylem cells that were able to transport water through the plant.

- **The fossil plant *Parka*** is also from the Devonian Period. Both *Cooksonia* and *Parka* probably reproduced with spores.

◀ *This reconstruction of* Cooksonia *shows its delicate branching stems and fruiting masses.*

▲ *These slender stems of* Cooksonia, *one of the first land plants, were found in rocks of Devonian age in Orkney, Scotland.*

- **Like many fossil plants**, these early Devonian species are preserved as thin carbon films, the rest of the plant tissue being lost during fossilization.

- **One of the best** examples of early plant preservation is a rock formation called the Rhynie chert, found in Devonian rocks in Scotland. Here, early plants are preserved three-dimensionally in silica.

- **Microscope analysis** of these silica fossils shows all their soft parts, allowing cellular structures to be examined.

- **It is probable that the Rhynie chert** was deposited by hot springs, the plant remains washing in from nearby.

Fossil plants and coal

- **When plants grow**, their energy is largely obtained from sunlight, which they use for photosynthesis and tissue development. This energy is locked away, but is released when coal formed from plants is burned.

- **Coal is formed** when plant material is buried, compressed, and heated.

- **The most important** deposits of coal, formed in the Carboniferous Period, occur in the UK, North America, Belgium, France, Australia, and Siberia.

- **Coal of Permian**, Triassic, and Jurassic age is important in China, Europe, and the USA. Coal from the Jurassic Period can be found in parts of the UK, especially northeast Scotland.

- **As coal is formed** from advanced land plants, no coal of any value built up before Carboniferous times, when vast forests grew in the swamps.

- **Carboniferous coal-forming forests** grew in warm, subtropical areas where rainfall was high, allowing rapid growth of giant horsetails and clubmosses.

- **The development** of brown, damp peat is the first stage in coal formation.

- **Peat is used as a fuel** in many parts of the world, but it doesn't burn at such a high temperature as coal.

- **In Ireland**, and many other countries including Russia, there are power plants that generate electricity by burning peat.

- **As peat is buried** under thousands of feet of sediment, it is heated and all impurities are removed. This increases the percentage of carbon, and turns the peat into coal.

▼ *Swamp forests, which produced coal, developed at many times in the past. This reconstruction shows a forest of Jurassic age.*

33

Coal-forming plants

- **The richest deposits of coal** have been formed by the accumulation of peat from forests. Coal-forming forests flourished in the Carboniferous Period.

- **As these forests grew** on the swampy top of vast deltas, they were flooded by the sea numerous times. This flooding brought sand and silt onto the deltas, in which fossil plants are often preserved.

- **A great variety of plants** grew in Carboniferous forests, including giant horsetails, clubmosses, and seed ferns.

- *Lepidodendron* is a common fossil clubmoss from Carboniferous strata. It grew to over 100 ft in height. The roots of this clubmoss are usually found as separate fossils, and are called *Stigmaria*.

- *Lepidodendron* stems can be recognized by their diamond-shaped leaf scars.

- **Another common** Carboniferous coal fossil is the giant horsetail, *Calamites*. Today, horsetails are relatively small plants that live in damp ground. *Calamites* grew to around 100 ft tall.

- **Horsetails** have soft tissue inside their stems, which decays rapidly when they die. During fossilization, the stems are often filled with sediment, so they are preserved in three dimensions.

- **A group of smaller plants** that helped make coal were called seed ferns.

- **Seed ferns** are plants with fernlike leaves, often preserved as carbon films on bedding planes.

- **Common Carboniferous** seed ferns include *Neuropteris*, *Eupecopteris*, and *Sphenopteris*.

▼ *These alternating coal, shale, and sandstone strata are on the coast of Fife, Scotland. The darker layers are coal made from plants that grew in the Carboniferous delta forests.*

Mazon Creek, Illinois

- **At certain times** in the fossil record a number of remarkably detailed accumulations of fossils occurred.

- **At Mazon Creek in Illinois**, coal has been strip-mined for many tens of years. Above the coal layers there are mudstones, in which rounded, iron-rich lumps, called nodules, occur.

- **Nodules like these** are common in mudstone and shale of different ages. Their importance is that fossils contained in them are often beautifully preserved in great detail.

- **It is thought** that these, and nodules in other strata, often form chemically around organic remains.

- **Plant fossils**, especially leaves, are commonly crushed on bedding planes, but in the Mazon Creek nodules, leaves are three-dimensional.

▶ *The delicate leaflets of the seed fern* Neuropteris *have been preserved as a carbon film inside an iron-stone nodule.*

◄ *None of the original carbon remains in this specimen of* Eupecopteris, *another seed fern. Nodules have to be opened very carefully to reveal such fossils.*

- **As well as perfect plants**, these rocks contain an amazing variety of other fossils, and geologists can work out the details of the habitats in which they lived.

- **Marine and freshwater** creatures are found here. Fossils of jellyfish (only preserved in ideal circumstances), worms, amphibians, and fish all occur in the Mazon Creek strata.

- **As often occurs** in cases of exceptional fossilization, there are fossils of soft-bodied creatures that are otherwise unknown.

- **Other examples** of nodules containing exceptional fossils are those from the Carboniferous rocks of Lancashire, UK, and the ammonite-bearing nodules of the British Lower Jurassic.

...FASCINATING FACT...
Spiders, scorpions, centipedes, and millipedes are fossilized at Mazon Creek, giving us a glimpse into a Carboniferous world that is unknown elsewhere.

Glossopteris and continental drift

- *Glossopteris* is an extinct seed fern. Its fossils occur in the southern landmasses of Antarctica, Australia, New Zealand, South America, and southern Africa.

- **This plant** had a treelike appearance and was up to 20 ft tall.

- **Usually only** the delicately veined leaves are found as fossils.

- **One of the most famous** geological books is *The Origins of Continents and Oceans*, written by Alfred Wegener, and published in 1924.

- **In this book**, Wegener puts together evidence to prove that the southern continents were at one time joined as a single landmass and have now drifted apart to their present positions.

- **Wegener was not a geologist** but a meteorologist, and his ideas were initially dismissed by the leading geologists of the time.

- **Because *Glossopteris*** occurs in the southern continents, which are now hundreds of miles away from each other, Wegener was able to use it as one of his key pieces of evidence to show that these areas had once been joined.

- **The problem** when he put forward his theory was that it was not understood how the continents could move.

- **Today**, we have the knowledge of plate tectonics, which shows how the ocean basins form and how the continents move, proving that Wegener was correct.

▶ Glossopteris *grew to around 20 ft in height. It may have grown with a treelike or bushy habit.*

● **The theory of plate tectonics** shows that the continents move at about one inch a year, the same speed at which your fingernails grow.

▲ *These iron-stained* Glossopteris *leaves are from Australia.*

Ginkgo and other living fossils

- **The expression "living fossil"** is often used to describe a plant or animal that occurs as a fossil in rocks formed many millions of years ago, and also lives today.

- **Living fossils** have been changed very little by evolution and have a very stable habitat and way of life.

- ***Ginkgo biloba***, the maidenhair tree, is grown in many countries, including the UK, as an ornamental tree, and is prized for its medicinal properties.

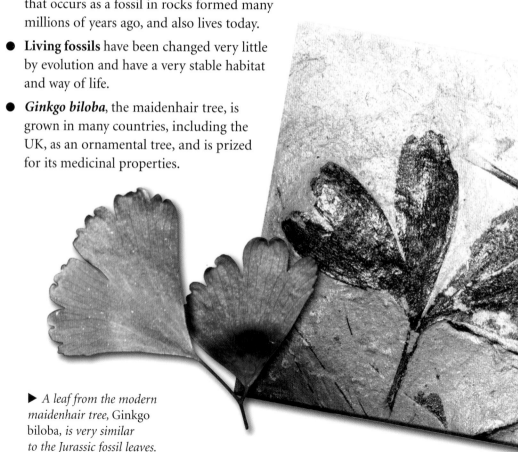

▶ *A leaf from the modern maidenhair tree,* Ginkgo biloba, *is very similar to the Jurassic fossil leaves.*

- **In China**, *Ginkgo* was cultivated in temple gardens as a sacred tree. It was thought to be extinct until some were found in the wild in southeast China in 1956.

- **Leaves of *Ginkgo***, usually preserved as carbon impressions, have been fossilized in rocks from the Permian Period (290–248 million years ago).

- **Fossilized *Ginkgo*** leaves are virtually the same as those of the living tree.

- **The leaves of** *Ginkgo* are very distinctive, being almost triangular in shape and partly indented.

- **Some of the best** *Ginkgo* fossils are from Jurassic strata on the coast of North Yorkshire, UK.

- **The brachiopod shellfish** *Lingula*, occurs in rocks of Cambrian age (545–495 million years ago). It is one of the earliest examples of a living fossil.

◄ *Leaves of* Ginkgo *from Jurassic strata in North Yorkshire, UK.*

...FASCINATING FACT...
Other well-known living fossils include the coelacanth, a fish thought to have been extinct for more than 60 million years until one was caught off South Africa in 1938.

Mesozoic and Cenozoic plants

- **Many ferns and fernlike plants** are fossilized in rocks formed during the Jurassic Period.

- *Coniopteris* is a fern found in Jurassic rocks. It occurs in North America, Europe, and Asia.

▼ *These delicate leaves are from the fernlike Jurassic plant, Williamsonia, which flourished in the swamp forests of the middle Jurassic Period.*

...FASCINATING FACT...
Flowers provide a way for plants to evolve, as pollen can combine
the genes of one plant with those of another.

- **Another common Jurassic** plant is *Williamsonia*. This is an extinct plant with fernlike leaves, which are usually preserved as black carbon films on bedding surfaces. It had cones rather than typical modern flowers.

- **The evolution** of flowering plants began toward the middle of the Mesozoic Era.

- **There is evidence** that plants with flower-like structures lived early in the Cretaceous Period (142–65 million years ago), but fossils of true flowers only occur toward the late Cretaceous.

- **Much of the evidence** that early plants bore flowers comes from fossil pollen.

- **Fossil pollen** is invaluable in helping to work out changes in the climate of the past.

- **The evolution of insects** is closely linked to the development of flowering plants. Insects feed on nectar and pollen, and carry pollen from flower to flower.

- **Fossil insects** are often perfectly preserved in amber, the hardened resin from pine and similar trees.

Fossil corals

- **Much limestone**, especially that deposited during the Paleozoic Era, consists of fossilized corals and coral fragments.

- **The earliest corals** are simple "tabulate" corals, which first appeared as fossils in rocks of the Ordovician Period.

- **Tabulate corals** have a tubular structure and may be attached to others to form a colony. The tube (corallite) is divided horizontally by sheets of calcite called tabulae.

- **The coral organism**, or polyp, was rather like a small sea anemone, and lived at the top of the tube.

- **Tabulate corals** became extinct in the Permian Period.

- *Dibunophyllum* belongs to a group called the "rugose" corals. These are more complex than the tabulate group.

- **In the Silurian** and Carboniferous Periods, rugose corals built large, shallow sea reefs, in which numerous fossils of corals, brachiopods, mollusks, crinoids, and trilobites are found.

  - **The rugose corals** became extinct at a similar time to the tabulate corals, in the Permian Period.

    - **Some corals** in the Carboniferous Period are used as zone fossils. Each coral species represents a small part of geological time.

      - **Modern corals** began to evolve early in the Mesozoic Era.

◀ *The delicate internal structure of corals is often well preserved in fossils, as seen in this species,* Dibunophyllum.

Lower Paleozoic corals

- **Tabulate and rugose corals** flourished during the Lower Paleozoic Era and at times built up large reefs.

- **Corals are easily fossilized**. They are made of calcium carbonate—the mineral calcite—which is stable in limestone. Also, they are solid structures, that are not easily eroded or broken.

- **Coral reefs** are good indicators of marine conditions and water depth. Their fossils help to reconstruct the ancient reef habitat.

- **Fossil mollusks**, brachiopods, trilobites, bryozoans, and crinoids are also found in rocks formed in these reef habitats.

- *Halysites* is a tabulate coral with a colonial structure. Its common name is chain coral because the individual corallites are linked together in a chain.

- **Lime mud** was easily trapped within the structure of corals such as *Halysites*, and so limestone was able to form.

- **Some tabulate corals** grew as large mounds on the shallow seabed. *Favosites* is a colonial coral, with numerous small corallites joined in a honeycomb structure, and is commonly known as honeycomb coral.

- **Both *Halysites* and *Favosites*** are common in reef limestones formed during the Silurian Period.

- **These corals** became extinct toward the end of the Devonian Period.

- *Halysites* and *Favosites* occur in many parts of the world including the UK, North America, Asia, and Australia, suggesting that shallow marine conditions were widespread.

▶ *A fossil of* Halysites, *a type of coral. Its chainlike structure is clearly visible.*

46

Time recording in the Paleozoic

- **Fossils can be used** to help reconstruct ancient habitats and to work out details about geological time, which can sometimes be verified by astronomers.

- **A study** of modern corals shows that they build up layers of calcite at regular times.

- **Within these calcite bands** there are thicker monthly and annual accumulations of calcite.

◀ *Growth bands in Ketophyllum shows that there were probably more than 400 days in the Silurian year.*

- **Fossil corals** are often preserved in great detail. This is because the calcite layers of which they are composed are very stable in limestone, and little altered. Many coral reefs are preserved almost as they lived.

- **A detailed analysis** of fossil corals shows considerable differences in the numbers of growth layers from modern corals.

- **The coral** *Ketophyllum*, which is fossilized in rocks of the Silurian Period, has 400 small growth bands between the wide annual markers.

- *Lithostrotion*, a common colonial coral found in Carboniferous rocks, has 398 growth bands per year.

- **There were**, as seen from the coral evidence, 400 days in the year during the Silurian Period, and 398 days in the year during the Carboniferous Period.

- **The relationship** between the Earth and the Sun has been changing through geological time. Corals prove that each day is now longer than in the past.

...FASCINATING FACT...
There are often 360 calcite secretions built up each year on modern corals, suggesting almost daily growth.

Jurassic reefs

- **The corals that evolved** during the Mesozoic Era, in the shallow sea reefs of the Jurassic Period, were different from those of the Paleozoic Era.

- **Jurassic corals** are classified as Scleractinian corals. They are also called hexacorals because they have six internal divisions.

- **Scleractinian corals** have many similarities to corals that live in tropical seas today.

- *Isastrea* **is a typical Jurassic coral that** flourished in warm, clear seawater with little mud suspended in it.

- **Modern tropical corals** require similar conditions—warm, clear water through which sunlight can penetrate.

- *Isastrea* grew as a mass of small, joined, individual corallites standing upright on the seabed.

- **When a lot of muddy sediment** was deposited, the coral reefs died out.

- **Lime mud** formed around corals that often derived from broken shells and other fossil debris. This then turned into limestone.

- **Many mollusks** thrived in this reef environment. Ammonite shells are also found in these limestones.

- **Other common fossils** in the reef rocks include brachiopods and burrows made by shrimps.

◄ *This specimen of* Isastrea, *from the Jurassic Period, shows the individual six-sided corallites.*

Fossil sponges

- **Sponges are mostly marine animals** that live in various habitats, and can be found today in low-shore rock pools.

- **Sponges are delicate organisms**. They are among the simplest multicelled creatures.

▶ *This modern tropical vase sponge has a feather star growing on it. Feather stars are closely related to starfish and sea urchins.*

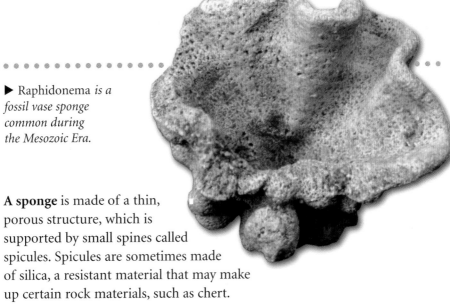

▶ Raphidonema *is a fossil vase sponge common during the Mesozoic Era.*

- **A sponge** is made of a thin, porous structure, which is supported by small spines called spicules. Spicules are sometimes made of silica, a resistant material that may make up certain rock materials, such as chert.

- **Surprisingly**, despite their structure, sponges are not uncommon as fossils.

- **Fossil sponges** occur mainly where sediment was deposited in a calm marine environment, with no strong currents.

- **Rocks** as old as the Cambrian Period contain fossil sponges.

- *Raphidonema* is a well-known fossil sponge found in Mesozoic rocks.

- **Some fossil sponges**, including *Siphonia*, have long stems and stand on the seabed. They look like tulips.

- *Raphidonema* has a structure like a porous, crinkled vase. It grew from the seabed, with its wide opening pointing upward.

- **Sponges form** part of a community of marine creatures. Often there are fossils of bivalve mollusks, such as oysters and pectens, and also gastropods and ammonites found with the fossil sponges.

Fossil crinoids

- **Crinoids are strange animals**, which have a plantlike structure. They have roots, a stem, and a cup (calyx) at the top, in which the animal lives.

- **Because of their structure**, crinoids are also called "sea lilies."

- **The solid parts** of the structure are made of calcite, which means crinoids are easily fossilized. However, it is usually only the stem that is preserved.

- **The stem is composed** of numerous small disks called ossicles. Before and during fossilization, the stem of a crinoid often breaks. Some crinoidal limestone is composed almost entirely of ossicles.

- **Above the calyx** are flexible, feathery arms. These direct water currents containing food toward the animal.

- **Crinoids** are closely related to starfish and sea urchins. All three groups of creatures belong to the phylum Echinodermata.

- *Traumatocrinus*, from the Triassic rocks of the Ghizou Province of China, shows the flexible stems and calyx with waving arms.

- **Crinoids** first evolved during the Ordovician Period.

- **Not all crinoids live** attached by their roots to the seabed. Some are free-swimming.

- **Today**, crinoids live in all depths of seawater. Some are even found in the deepest abyssal water.

▶ *Each of these specimens of* Traumatocrinus *has a calyx, stem, and arms.*

Encrinus and the Triassic of Germany

- *Encrinus* is one of the best-preserved fossil crinoids. It reveals a lot about crinoids and their way of life.

- **During the Triassic Period**, much of Germany was covered by the sea. This was in great contrast to the dry, desertlike conditions that existed in Britain at that time.

- **Part of this German sea** is called the Muschelkalk. This name refers to the limestone, rich in fossil shells, which formed there.

- **Crinoid fossils**, especially Encrinus, are abundant in the Muschelkalk limestones.

- **An important feature** of these fossils is the excellent preservation of the upper structure of the crinoids, the calyx.

- *Encrinus* has a perfect fivefold symmetry, as do many of the members of their phylum.

Calyx made of larger plates

Arms made of smaller
interlocking plates

- **Among its close relatives** are starfish and sea urchins.

- **These crinoids** have been studied for hundreds of years, and the name *Encrinus* was first used in the 16th century.

- **By comparing *Encrinus*** with living crinoids, its way of life can be suggested.

- ***Encrinus*** probably lived in flowing sea currents, with its calyx pointing into the current. This allowed food particles to be easily carried toward the animal.

◀ *This typical specimen of* Encrinus *shows the calyx made of large plates, with the arms made of smaller interlocking plates, folded tightly above.*

Jurassic crinoids

▲ *The slender arms of this specimen of* Pentacrinus *have been preserved in pyrite (fool's gold).*

- **During the Jurassic Period**, shallow seas existed at certain times in many areas, including Britain.

- **The crinoid *Pentacrinus*** is found fossilized in the limestones that were formed on this shallow seabed.

- *Pentacrinus* is well-known for the structure of its stem. The small ossicles, of which it is made, are star shaped. Because the stem is very brittle, these small stars are often all that is fossilized of the whole crinoid.

- **As well as being found** in limestones, *Pentacrinus* occurs in the dark mudstones formed in deeper parts of the Jurassic sea.

- **It has been suggested** that *Pentacrinus* may have lived on driftwood and other debris, as well as on the seabed. This could explain how it reached deeper water.

- **Modern species** of *Pentacrinus* are anchored to the seabed when they are young. As they mature, they break away and become free-swimming.

- *Pentacrinus* has very long arms rising above the small calyx. These arms branch many times.

- **When found fossilized** in dark mudstones and shales, *Pentacrinus* is often preserved in iron pyrite. This is an iron sulphide mineral with a glistening golden color. It is known as "fool's gold."

- **Many other fossils** are found in the same strata as *Pentacrinus*. These include various mollusks, brachiopods, and other echinoderms.

- **From a study of the rock** in which these fossils are found, and of the fossils themselves, the habitat can be reconstructed.

Brittle stars

- **Brittle stars** are delicate starfish with long, slender arms. Usually, there are five arms, giving them typical echinoderm symmetry.

- **As in other starfish**, the animal's mouth is in the central disk. The flexible arms allow the creature to move rapidly over the seabed.

- **Many brittle stars** feed on plankton, but some species eat small shellfish.

- **Fossils** of brittle stars, which are scientifically called ophiuroids, are found in rocks dating as far back as the Ordovician Period.

- **There are a number** of "starfish beds" in the fossil record, some of the best being found in lower Jurassic rocks.

- **Other numbers** of brittle stars have been found in Devonian rocks in Germany and Silurian strata in Scotland.

- **Today**, brittle stars often live in large numbers in both shallow and deep seas.

- **Because brittle stars are so delicate**, the possibility of them being washed together by sea currents and fossilized as a large number of perfect specimens, is remote.

- **For a mass of brittle stars** to be fossilized together, it is likely that a colony was rapidly covered with mud or sand.

- **It has been discovered** that living brittle stars cannot escape from sediment more than 2 in deep.

▶ *This fossil mass of brittle stars shows the central disk and flexible arms, all with fivefold symmetry.*

Jurassic sea urchins

- **Sea urchins** (echinoids) have evolved into many forms that are closely related to their habitat.

- **Regular echinoids** generally have a rounded shell (test). The mouthpart is positioned at the bottom of the shell, and the anus is positioned at the top.

- **The shell** is made of five bands of plates, which give it a fivefold symmetry. Spines are attached to the outside of the shell, and thin, delicate tube feet protrude through pores. The spines and tube feet are used for movement.

- **Irregular echinoids** have a similar structure but the shell has a twofold symmetry.

▲ *This echinoid is called a "pencil urchin" because of the size and shape of its spines. The ball-and-socket joints where they join the shell (test) are clearly seen.*

Hundreds of years ago in Oxfordshire, UK, fossils of *Clypeus* were referred to as pound stones and used as a measure of weight.

- **Some echinoids** are flattened, such as *Clypeus*, while others are dome-shaped.

- *Clypeus* is a relatively large fossil sea urchin at about 4 in in diameter.

- *Clypeus* has petal-shaped bands of plates running around its shell.

  - **Modern sand dollars** are flattened echinoids, with similar shells to *Clypeus*. They live on or in the seabed in calm seawater.

    - *Clypeus* often occurs in oolitic limestone of Jurassic age. It is often fossilized with mollusks and brachiopods.

◄ Clypeus *is an irregular sea urchin. Its spines were probably removed by sea currents before it was fossilized.*

Spiny sea urchins

- **Sea urchins** use their spines for moving about and as protection from predators.

- **The spines** on sea urchins vary greatly. Some echinoids have a few stout, club-shaped spines and others have a mass of slender, pointed spines.

- *Cidaris* is a fossil sea urchin from rocks of Jurassic to Recent age.

- **On its shell**, *Cidaris* has large, rounded "bosses" where the spines were attached with a ball-and-socket joint.

- **Often the shell breaks** up during fossilization, and the large spines are frequently found as individual fossils.

- *Cidaris* **has a rounded shell** with the mouth centrally positioned on its underside, and is classified as a regular echinoid.

- **In rocks of Jurassic age**, *Cidaris* is found in limestone strata with many other fossils. These include corals, brachiopods, mollusks, and bryozoans.

▶ Psammechinus, *also known as the green sea urchin, is a modern sea urchin with many thin, sharp spines.*

- **Psammechinus** is a spiny sea urchin that lives today in shallow seas, and can be found in rock pools on the shore at low tide.

- **The spines** on *Psammechinus* are relatively large. They are attached to the outside of the shell in a similar way to those on the fossil *Cidaris*.

- **As with fossil sea urchins**, the spines break off *Psammechinus* when it dies. Empty shells washed up on the shore rarely have spines attached to them.

◀ *Delicate echinoid spines are rarely preserved as fossils. The Jurassic sea urchin* Cidaris *is very similar to the modern-day* Psammechinus.

Burrowing sea urchins

- **Sea urchins** that burrow into the soft sediment on the seabed are often heart-shaped in outline.

- *Micraster* is a common fossil sea urchin. It is found in chalk formed in the Cretaceous Period.

- **Because of its unusual outline**, *Micraster* is classified as an irregular echinoid.

- **Other features** that make it irregular are its very short, petal-shaped rows of plates, and the noncentral position of the mouth and anus.

- *Micraster* has been the subject of many scientific studies. An evolutionary sequence of this genus has been worked out.

- **The chalk** in which fossils of *Micraster* are found, was formed as a fine mud on the seabed.

▲ *This specimen of the Cretaceous sea urchin,* Micraster *has the typical heart-shaped outline of a burrowing echinoid.*

- **Other fossils** found with *Micraster* include bivalve mollusks, sponges, corals, brachiopods, and fish teeth.

- *Echinocardium* is a modern sea urchin that lives in shallow seas. It burrows into mud and sand.

- **This recent sea urchin** has a heart-shaped shell, very similar to that of *Micraster.*

- **Although *Echinocardium* is covered** with soft spines when alive, dead shells washed up on the shore are usually bare of spines.

◄ Echinocardium *is a common echinoid around the coast of Britain. Its scientific name means "spiny heart." It is a burrower, like the fossil* Micraster.

Brachiopods

- **Brachiopods** are marine shellfish that are very different from other shelled animals. They are classified in a phylum of their own and are commonly known as lampshells.

- **A typical brachiopod** has a shell made of two valves. Some brachiopods are able to open and close their shells to let in seawater containing food.

- **The two valves** of a brachiopod shell differ from each other. One valve has a hole in its pointed end through which a tough stalk sticks out. This stalk, called the pedicle, anchors the animal to the seabed.

- **Inarticulate brachiopods** are the most primitive, and were first found fossilized in Ordovician strata.

- *Lingula* is an inarticulate brachiopod, as it can't open and close its shell.

- **This brachiopod** burrows vertically into soft mud on the seabed.

- **Modern-day** *Lingula* can help paleontologists suggest what habitat this brachiopod lived in before they became fossilized

- **Primitive brachiopods**, such as *Lingula,* have different shell compositions from other brachiopods. *Lingula*'s shell is made of phosphates and chitin—a similar material to human fingernails.

- *Lingula* is found fossilized in dark shales and mudstones with other brachiopods and bivalve mollusks.

...FASCINATING FACT...
Lingula is called a living fossil because it has remained
virtually unchanged for 500 million years.

▲ *These shells of Lingula are preserved
in strata of Ordovician age.*

Paleozoic brachiopods

- **Brachiopods** still live today, but they were far more numerous in the past than they are now.

- **During the Carboniferous Period**, many brachiopods, including *Spirifer* and *Productus*, lived in the shallow seas that covered much of Europe and North America.

- *Spirifer* **and** *Productus* are called articulate brachiopods because they could open and close their shells.

- **The symmetry** of a brachiopod shell is different to that of a bivalve mollusk. A bivalve has two valves that are similar to each other. A brachiopod's two valves differ from each other.

- *Spirifer* has a small shell crossed with thick ridges called ribs. There is a straight hinge line along which the shell opens.

- *Productus* is a different shape from *Spirifer*. It is more rounded, and some species grew quite large. *Gigantoproductus* commonly grew to 6 in in width.

▲ *This specimen of* Spirifer *from Carboniferous limestone shows the straight hinge line and radiating ribs.*

- **The shell** of *Productus* is covered with circular growth lines and thin radiating ribs.

- ***Productus*** often has a spiny shell, although the delicate spines break off easily during fossilization. These spines may have helped to anchor the shell in mud on the seabed.

- **Both of these brachiopods** are commonly found in limestone of the Carboniferous Period.

- **Other fossils** found with *Productus* and *Spirifer* include corals, trilobites, and mollusks.

▶ Productus *is a common fossil brachiopod. A few of the spines used to anchor the shell into the mud of the seabed can be seen here.*

Spines

Rhynchonellids

- **Small brachiopods** with heavily ribbed shells are common in many Jurassic strata. These are classified as Rhynchonellids.

- **The shell** of a typical Rhynchonellid is only about 2 in in diameter.

- **They are articulate brachiopods**, which could open and close their shells. The larger pedicle valve has a hole from which the fleshy pedicle protruded.

- **The shell** is made of calcite, unlike the phosphatic shell of the inarticulate brachiopods.

- **This group** seems to have been very successful, and first evolved during the Ordovician Period. Some species still live today.

- **A notable feature** of the shell is the zigzag line along which the shell opens.

- **These brachiopods** are found in a number of different Jurassic strata. They are most common in limestones and ironstones, and also occur in sandstones.

KEY

1 Thecosmilia
2 Chlamys
3 Rhynchonellids
4 Rhabdophyllia
5 Bryozoan
6 Cladophyllia conybeari
7 Trochid

- **They are fossilized** with ammonites and other mollusks, crinoids, echinoids, and other types of brachiopods.

- **Rhynchonellids are often** fossilized in small clusters. It is probable that they lived attached in groups to the seabed.

- **From the strata** in which they are fossilized, it can be worked out that these brachiopods preferred clear seawater, without much sand or mud.

▲ *Small Rhynchonellid brachiopods lived attached to the seabed. In this reef habitat, numerous other organisms were common, including corals, mollusks, and echinoids.*

Terebratulids

- **Although abundant** in Jurassic strata, the Terebratulid brachiopods have a very long geological history. They are still alive today, and the earliest fossils of them are found in Ordovician strata.

- **A typical Terebratulid** has an oval shell that is about 1–2 in in length.

- **Often the shell is smooth**, without obvious ribs. Growth lines, which show the edge of the shell when it was smaller, can usually be seen.

- **One valve** is bigger than the other. This, the pedicle valve, has a hole for the pedicle.

- **Terebratulids**, like other articulate brachiopods, feed on material suspended in seawater. A current of water enters the shell when it is slightly opened.

- **Inside a brachiopod shell** is a structure called the brachidium. This is sometimes found in fossils. Its purpose was to support the main food-gathering organ, the feathery lophophore.

- **Terebratulid brachiopods** occur in a variety of Jurassic strata. However, they are most common in certain limestones.

- **Oolitic limestone** is a common rock formed in the Jurassic Period. It is made of minute, rounded grains of calcite that form in moving seawater.

- **Unlike the Rhynchonellids**, the Terebratulids occur individually, and seem not to have clustered in masses.

> ...FASCINATING FACT...
> Fossils found with Terebratulids include ammonites and other
> mollusks, corals, echinoids, and crinoids.

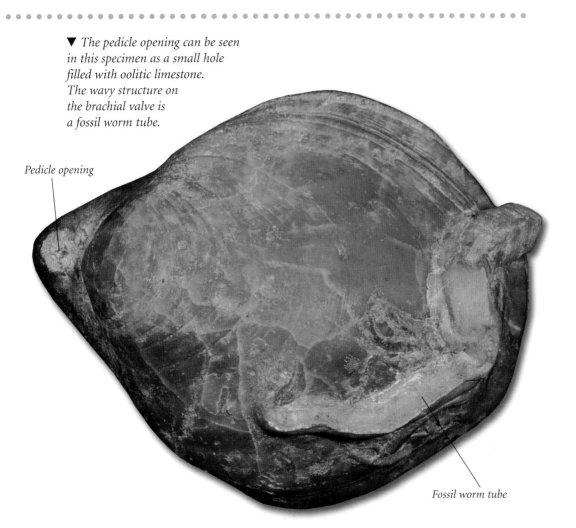

▼ *The pedicle opening can be seen in this specimen as a small hole filled with oolitic limestone. The wavy structure on the brachial valve is a fossil worm tube.*

Pedicle opening

Fossil worm tube

Graptolites

- **Graptolites** were simple marine animals that first appeared in the Cambrian Period. They became extinct in the Carboniferous Period.

- **Graptolite** fossils are found in rocks that formed in the deep sea, such as dark mudstones and shales. The name "graptolite" means "writing in stone."

- **A typical graptolite**, such as *Didymograptus,* has a slender, elongated structure, often only 1–2 in in length. This is called the stipe.

- **When examined in detail**, a graptolite's stipe has a series of small projections on one or both sides, giving the appearance of the teeth found on a saw. These are called thecae and in life, were small cups in which tiny marine creatures called zooids lived.

- **The graptolite** is the structure built up by a colony of zooids and was either anchored to the seabed, or in other cases, it floated along on ocean currents.

- **Originally**, graptolites were classified with small colonial marine organisms called hydrozoans. In the 1940s, their classification was reorganized when their biology was closely examined.

- **Graptolites are classified** in their own phylum, the Hemichordata, which also includes acorn worms and pterobranchs.

- **Because they are so delicate**, graptolites are preserved in only the finest-grained sedimentary rocks. They often occur in great masses, looking like pencil marks on the bedding planes.

- **Sometimes**, they are preserved in iron pyrite, and three-dimensional preservation occurs in rare cases.

- *Didymograptus* is found in strata of Ordovician age.

▲ Didymograptus *can be identified by the "V" shaped position of the two stipes. The saw-tooth thecae are on the inside of the "V."*

Graptolites and geological time

- **Although graptolites** are very delicate organisms, they are geographically widespread in certain strata from the Lower Paleozoic Era.

- **Graptolites evolved** into many different species and in some, rocks are very common fossils.

- **A sequence of strata** has been established using graptolites as relative time markers (zone fossils). *Monograptus* is used as a zone fossil for rocks of the Silurian Period.

- ***Monograptus*** has a single stipe, with thecae only on one side giving it the appearance of a miniature hacksaw.

- **Graptolites** with thecae only on one side of the stipe are called uniserial graptolites. If the thecae are on both sides, they are called biserial graptolites.

- **Graptolites**, such as *Monograptus*, are believed to have been planktonic, carried by sea currents, while possibly attached to floating material.

Orthograptus   *Dictyonema*

- **It is possible** that many planktonic graptolites would have drifted into areas where coarse sediment was deposited. Because graptolites are so delicate they would have been crushed and destroyed as these rocks formed.

- **In some areas**, many thousands of *Monograptus* are fossilized on single bedding planes.

- **Some of the best-preserved** graptolites have been found in Silurian rocks in Germany and Poland. These rocks occur as boulders, slowly carried by glaciers from the bed of the Baltic Sea.

- **Perfectly preserved** graptolites can be removed from these boulders by dissolving pieces of the rock in acid.

▼ *Many different types of graptolites evolved. Some had single stipes, like* Monograptus, *others joined together in a colony, like* Dictyonema.

Monograptus   *Phyllograptus*   *Loganograptus*   **79**

Arthropods

- **Arthropods** are one of the most varied and successful groups of creatures to have evolved.

- **The first arthropods** are found fossilized in rocks of Cambrian age. They are still numerous in all manner of habitats today.

- **The scientific name** for the arthropod group is phylum Arthropoda. It contains creatures that can fly, swim, burrow, and sting.

- **Butterflies and moths**, crabs and lobsters, shrimps, centipedes, spiders, and scorpions, are all arthropods.

- **These creatures** have a tough outer skin (exoskeleton) that protects and holds together the soft body.

- **As an arthropod grows**, it sheds its exoskeleton. Many pass through a larval stage, and molt as the larva grows.

- **Some arthropods have claws**, others wings, and most have segmented legs and thin, flexible feelers.

Feeler

Claw

Leg

- **Perhaps the best-known** fossil arthropods are the trilobites. Many trilobite fossils may be the remains of shed exoskeletons.

- *Eryon* is a marine arthropod that probably lived on the seabed.

- **Many arthropods** have excellent vision. Trilobites were the first known animals to have complex eyes that could form detailed images.

▲ Eryon *is an arthropod from Jurassic strata. It was an early member of the crab and lobster group, Decapoda. The segmented exoskeleton, legs, feelers, and claws have been perfectly preserved.*

Giant sea scorpions

- **During the Paleozoic Era**, arthropods called eurypterids (giant sea scorpions) terrorized the seabed.

- **The first eurypterids** appeared in the Ordovician Period, and became extinct in the Permian Period.

- **The largest eurypterid** grew to 6 ft in length. However, some were just 4 in long.

- **These arthropods** had a tough outer skeleton, which they molted as they grew.

- **The body was long and flexible**, and had six pairs of limbs. The pair nearest the tail were paddle-shaped, and were probably used for moving through the water.

▼ Pterygotus, *a giant sea scorpion, had good vision, and large claws for grasping prey. At least one pair of limbs was adapted for swimming.*

▲ *This fossil sea scorpion,* Baltoeurypterus, *is from Silurian rocks in the Ukraine. It is shown here at life-size.*

- **The head was small**, and some kinds had huge, elongated claws extending from it.
- **Eurypterids** were good swimmers and relied on their long claws to grab prey.
- **Compound eyes** allowed these creatures to detect and catch their prey.
- **As well as** marine eurypterids, many other species also lived in brackish water or freshwater.

Fossil insects

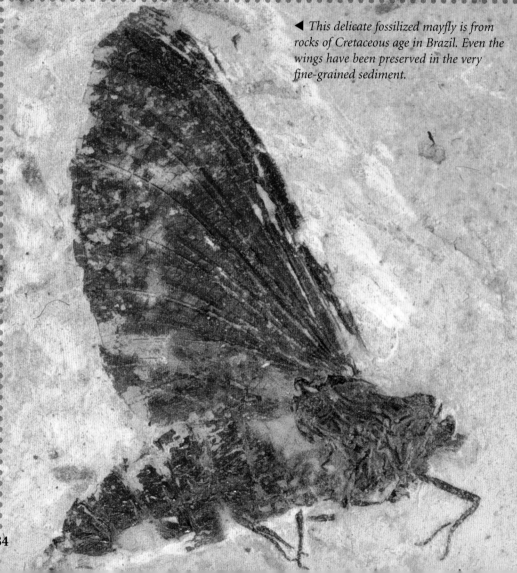

◀ This delicate fossilized mayfly is from rocks of Cretaceous age in Brazil. Even the wings have been preserved in the very fine-grained sediment.

- **Insects** have all the main features of the arthropods. Many of them are also able to fly.

- **Even though they are delicate**, insects have a tough exoskeleton. For this reason, the fossil record of insects is surprisingly good.

- **Insects often need** special circumstances to become fossilized. Very fine-grained, dustlike sediment helps to preserve delicate details.

- **Many insects** have been preserved in amber—the hardened resin that oozes from pine and similar trees. Insects that got stuck in the resin could become perfectly fossilized.

- **Because many insects** live on land, their fossils are less common than sea dwelling arthropods.

- **Insects** first appeared as fossils in rocks of Devonian age.

- **During the Carboniferous Period**, giant dragonflies flew over the swamps that covered much of Europe and North America.

- **Some insects** pass through various stages of development (metamorphosis). Fossils of caterpillars and chrysalids have been found in rocks of Mesozoic age.

- **The first insects** were probably predators. When flowering plants developed in the Mesozoic Era, they provided pollen and nectar as food for many insects. In turn, insects carried pollen from flower to flower and helped fertilize plants.

- **It has been suggested** that insect DNA could be recovered from fossils in amber. This is highly unlikely as the chemical structure of DNA breaks down quickly.

Fossil crabs

- **As with other arthropods**, crabs have a hard outer skeleton, which molts as they grow.

- **The legs**, feelers, and claws are attached underneath the body. Here, there is less exoskeleton and the crab may be more vulnerable to attack from predators.

- **Modern-day king crabs** are not crustaceans, but chelicerates and are related to spiders and scorpions. They have a structure that is similar to that of the trilobites.

- *Mesolimulus* is a fossil king crab from Jurassic strata in southern Germany. It is very similar to certain modern king crabs.

- **The limestones** at Solnhofen, in which this and other delicate fossils have been preserved, are one of the most famous fossil deposits.

- **Other creatures** fossilized here include jellyfish, worms, and arthropods, such as shrimps and insects.

- *Mesolimulus* has a long tail spine and curved head shield.

- **Curved compound eyes** are positioned on each side of the head shield, and there are claws at the front.

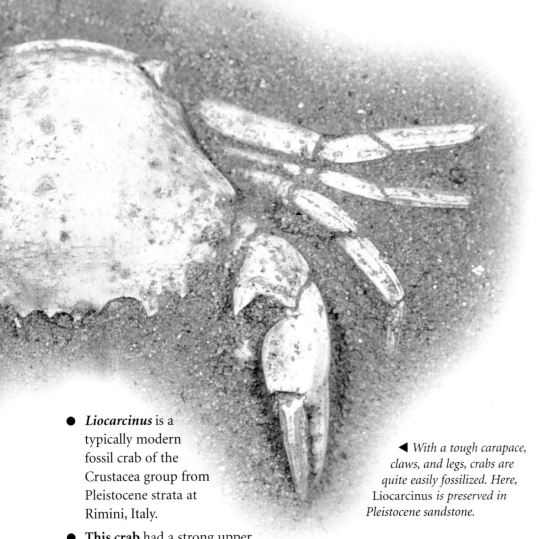

● *Liocarcinus* is a
typically modern
fossil crab of the
Crustacea group from
Pleistocene strata at
Rimini, Italy.

◀ *With a tough carapace,
claws, and legs, crabs are
quite easily fossilized. Here,
Liocarcinus is preserved in
Pleistocene sandstone.*

● **This crab** had a strong upper
exoskeleton, often called the
carapace, which allowed it to be preserved in sandstone.

Giant trilobites

- **Trilobites** are probably the best-known group of fossil arthropods. They are first found in rocks from the Cambrian Period.

- **Along with many different creatures**, trilobites became extinct during the Permian Period.

- **Trilobites** were advanced marine creature with a complex, three-lobed structure. They had a central axis and two lateral lobes, hence the name trilobite, which means three lobes.

- **They had a head shield** (cephalon) that, in many types including *Paradoxides*, had eyes. The central nervous system was probably here. *Paradoxides* had long spines extending back from the edges of the head shield.

- **The exoskeleton** was flexible, and *Paradoxides* was able to move across the seabed using legs attached underneath.

- ***Paradoxides*** was a much larger trilobite. Its fossilized remains occur in Cambrian rocks in Europe, North and South America, and north Africa. It is used as a zone fossil to date rocks relatively.

- **It is a puzzle** to paleontologists why creatures as complex and advanced as trilobites have no apparent ancestors. They are present in the Cambrian strata, but not before that.

- **Precambrian rocks** are often metamorphosed and altered, so any fossils in them would have been destroyed. However, there are marine sedimentary strata of late Precambrian times without any trace of trilobites in them.

- **Their ancestors** may have been soft-bodied creatures, which could not have become fossilized. Trilobites probably developed exoskeletons early in the Cambrian Period, and then would have been readily fossilized.

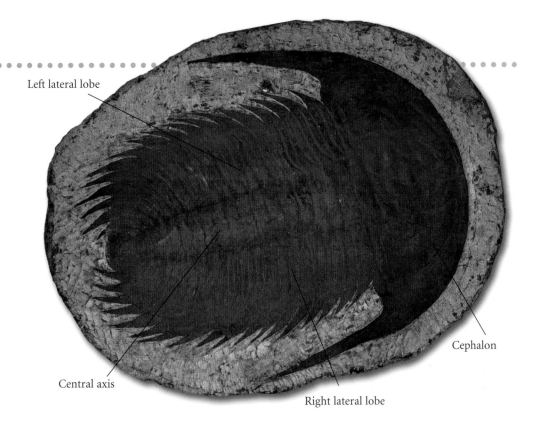

Left lateral lobe

Central axis

Right lateral lobe

Cephalon

▲ *This specimen of* Paradoxides *comes from early Cambrian strata in Morocco.*

...FASCINATING FACT...
Most trilobites were about 2 in or less in length.
Paradoxides grew much larger, some giants were up to 24 in long.

Silurian trilobites

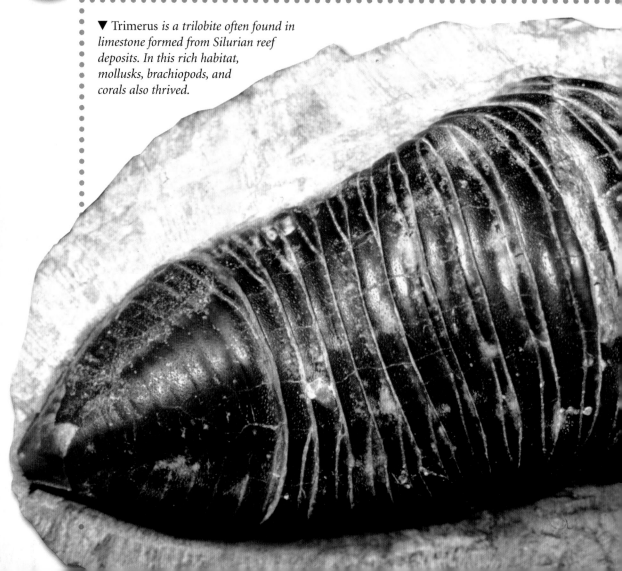

▼ Trimerus *is a trilobite often found in* *limestone formed from Silurian reef* *deposits. In this rich habitat,* *mollusks, brachiopods, and* *corals also thrived.*

- **During the Silurian Period,** shallow marine conditions with reefs existed at certain times.

- **These reefs** were built up of lime-rich sediment that was bound together by many organisms, including corals and bryozoans. Between the reefs, limestone strata formed.

- **Conditions** at the time were favorable for many different organisms, and these rocks are rich in a variety of fossils. There are brachiopods, corals, mollusks, and trilobites.

- *Trimerus* is an unusual trilobite from Silurian limestone. It has a very smooth carapace (upper exoskeleton) and the three-lobed structure is not easy to see.

- **The head shield** has a triangular outline, and there are no eyes.

- **The smooth** exoskeleton and lack of eyes suggest that *Trimerus* may have burrowed into the seabed mud.

- *Dalmanites* was a small Ordovician and Silurian trilobite, which had eyes raised above the head shield.

- **Trilobites with raised eyes** may have had good all-around vision. They may also have burrowed into the mud on the seabed with their eyes protruding.

- *Dalmanites* has a typical trilobite structure, with three lobes and obvious head, thorax, and tail sections.

- **In some species** of *Dalmanites* the tail section (pygidium) ends in a sharp spine.

Trilobite defense

- **The flexible outer skeleton** of many arthropods allows them considerable movement and some can roll up completely.

- *Calymene* is a trilobite from Silurian and Devonian rocks, and has many typical trilobite characteristics.

- **A strange feature** of *Calymene* is the two rounded projections on each side of the glabella (the central part of the head shield).

- **This trilobite** genus has a wide head shield, a typically three-lobed thorax, and a small tail section.

- **As well as being found** as usual trilobite fossils, enrolled specimens of *Calymene* and other trilobites have been found.

- **Many arthropods**, including woodlice (pillbugs), can be found enrolled with their hard carapaces protecting the softer parts hidden inside.

- **Like modern arthropods**, trilobites were probably able to enroll their bodies.

- **This action** provides a defence from predators. However, being enrolled probably wouldn't have saved a trilobite from a large predator.

- **It has been suggested** that when they were rolled up, trilobites would be able to save energy if food was not easily obtained.

- **Certain grooves** found on the bedding planes of some sedimentary rocks have been described as trilobite trails. In the USA, specimens of *Calymene* have been found near these grooves.

◄ *Trilobites may have rolled up in self defence. In this position, the tough exoskeleton is outermost, protecting the softer body parts.*

Butterfly stones

▲ *A winged tail section (pygidium) of* Drepanura. *This limestone is also crowded with fragments of other fossils.*

- **Many trilobite exoskeletons** break up before they are fossilized. This usually happens between the head shield and thorax, and the thorax and pygidium (tail).

- **Molted trilobite exoskeletons** may account for many of the fossils found. These may have broken as the trilobite wriggled out.

- **Fossil specimens** of *Drepanura* are usually only the tail sections. Only rarely are other parts of the animal found.

- **These fossils** are a very strange shape. They have a central section of small, toothlike spines and two extended spines on the edges.

- **Rocks containing** *Drepanura* often have many broken fragments of other fossils.

- *Drepanura* had eyes on its head shield.

- **Rocks** containing these fossils are often called "butterfly stones" because of the winged shape of the pygidium.

- *Drepanura* is one of the earliest trilobites to be found in the fossil record, occurring in strata of Cambrian age.

- **As well as being found in China**, *Drepanura* also occurs in Cambrian strata in Europe.

...FASCINATING FACT...

Hundreds of years ago, probably before anyone knew what these strange shapes in the rocks were, they were collected and used by Chinese doctors. The Chinese called them "Hu-die-shih."

Very small trilobites

- *Agnostus* is one of the earliest trilobites, occurring in strata of Cambrian age.

- **As well as being a very small trilobite**, up to 0.5 in long, *Agnostus* has some unusual features.

- **This trilobite** has only two segments making up its thorax. The head shield and tail are both semicircular.

- *Agnostus* had no eyes on the head shield.

- **In some areas**, great masses of broken exoskeletons of *Agnostus* are preserved as fossils.

- **Some of the most amazing Cambrian fossils** come from the Burgess Shale of British Columbia and Vastergotland in Sweden. In these areas, masses of strange, soft-bodied creatures and large numbers of crustaceans are preserved. These give us an idea of what life in the Cambrian sea was really like.

- **The predominance** of fossil trilobites in Cambrian rocks, including *Agnostus*, is probably a result of their hard exoskeletons being more easily preserved than the remains of soft-bodied creatures.

- **Fossils of *Agnostus*** have been found rolled up like woodlice.

- **In well-preserved fossils** from Sweden, *Agnostus* trilobites have been found with an unusual appendage. This has made some paleontologists wonder if *Agnostus* really is a trilobite.

- ***Agnostus* usually occurs** with fossils of other trilobites, mollusks, and graptolites.

▶ *A mass of fragments of* Agnostus *trilobites preserved in limestone. Their typical length was about 0.5 in.*

Trilobite vision

- **Trilobites first appeared** in the Cambrian Period and unlike many of the creatures of the time, some were able to see.

- **Fossilized eyes** may seem a little strange as eyes are soft and decay rapidly after death. However, trilobites' eyes were made of calcite (calcium carbonate) and could be easily fossilized.

- **Calcite** is a common mineral, which is found in many rocks, especially limestone. Under the right conditions, it can remain for millions of years in the Earth's crust without being changed.

- **Trilobites** are related to many modern creatures with excellent eyesight, such as dragonflies, flies, wasps, bees, crabs, and lobsters.

- **Like many modern-day insects**, trilobites had compound eyes.

- **Human eyes** only have one lens, but compound eyes have many lenses all joined together.

- **Compound eyes** are excellent for seeing movement. For example, modern-day dragonflies can see smaller insects flying nearby and can suddenly change direction to catch them.

- **Scientists** have tried to work out what a trilobite could see with its compound eyes. Many species probably had very good vision.

- **Some trilobites** had eyes on stalks extending from the head shield. They may have lived on the seabed, with their eyes sticking out of the mud-like periscopes.

- **Not all trilobites had eyes.** Some used feelers and grooves in their exoskeleton for detecting the movement of water currents and finding their way about.

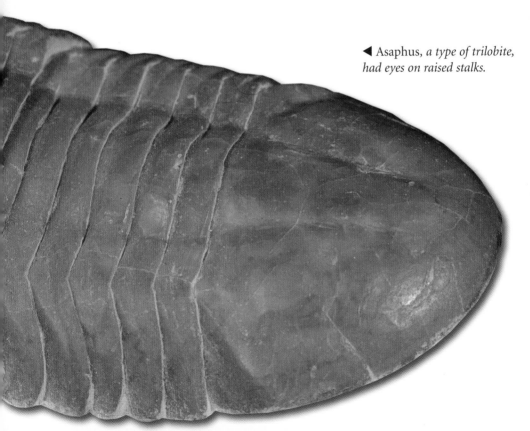

◀ Asaphus, *a type of trilobite, had eyes on raised stalks.*

Continental drift and trilobites

- **The theory of continental drift** suggests that the large land masses (continents) are constantly moving. At times during the past they have been joined together, but now many are separate.

- **A number of fossils** have been used to prove this theory, including the trilobite *Olenellus*. It can help to show that Scotland and North America were once joined together.

- **This trilobite** can be found in rocks from the Cambrian Period.

- **During the Cambrian Period**, North America and Scotland were joined. A deep ocean separated this area from Wales, and *Olenellus* was unable to move across it.

- **Although there are many places** where Cambrian trilobites occur in Britain, *Olenellus* is only found in northwest Scotland.

- *Olenellus* is also fossilized in Cambrian rocks in North America.

- **The rocks** in which *Olenellus* is found were probably formed in relatively shallow marine conditions. These rocks include limestone and mudstone.

- **The main feature** that distinguishes *Olenellus* from other trilobites is its spines, which extend from the head shield and from the sides of the thorax and tail.

- *Olenellus* had large, curved eyes on the sides of the head shield.

- **It is an example** of an advanced Cambrian creature with no obvious Precambrian ancestors.

▶ *A fossilized* Olenellus *trilobite from Cambrian rocks.*

Mollusks

- **Today**, mollusks live in a great variety of habitats. They are very important fossils, occurring as far back as Cambrian times.

- **Mollusks can live** in both saltwater and freshwater. Some live on land, and some even climb trees. Fossil mollusks are good indicators of the habitat in which a layer of rock was deposited.

- **The word "mollusk"** refers to creatures that have a soft, slimy body, which may or may not have a shell around it.

- **Octopuses**, slugs and snails, clams and oysters, squids and cuttlefish, and tusk shells are also mollusks.

- **Scientifically**, the phylum Mollusca is divided into smaller groups called classes. Among the main classes are the Gastropoda, Bivalvia, and Cephalopoda.

- **Some gastropods** (Gastropoda) can live in water, others on land. They are slugs, snails, and limpets. This class is not as common in the fossil record as the other mollusks.

- **Bivalves** (Bivalvia) live in both saltwater and freshwater. Some bivalves, such as *Mya* (types of clam), burrow into sand and mud. *Pecten* (the scallop) can open and close its valves to swim, and oysters lie on the seabed.

- **The cephalopods** (Cephalopoda) are marine animals. They are among the most intelligent invertebrates, with a well-developed nervous system and sensitive eyes. Octopus, squid, cuttlefish, and the pearly nautilus are in this class.

- **The ammonites**, one of the best-known groups of fossils, are classified as mollusks and belong to the class Cephalopoda.

- **Mollusks are common** as fossils, sometimes occurring in such large numbers that they make up most of a sedimentary rock.

◀ *Ammonites are one of the best-known groups of extinct mollusks. They are common in strata of Mesozoic age.*

Bivalve mollusks that swim

◀ *This image shows the soft body of a scallop shell between the two valves. When the valves open and close, the animal swims in short bursts.*

● **These mollusks** are called bivalves because they have a shell made of two, usually similar, valves, which are a mirror image of each other.

● **Near the rounded** or pointed "beak" of the shell (the umbo) there is a dark, horny, flexible ligament that holds the two valves together.

● **Just below the umbo**, on the insides of the shell, is a series of ridges (teeth) and hollows (sockets). Teeth in one valve fit into sockets in the other valve and, together with the ligament, they make a hinge system.

● **Inside the shell**, the animal's body is surrounded by a fleshy membrane called the mantle.

● **Two strong muscles**, the adductor muscles, pull the valves together. When they relax, the valves open slightly.

● **Features of the many** fossil species of bivalves differ, often depending on the habitat in which the creature lived.

● *Pseudopecten*, from the Jurassic Period, and the modern *Pecten* (scallop) have one large adductor muscle. Although they are separated by many millions of years, their features are very similar.

- **These two bivalves** open and shut their valves using the large adductor muscle. This causes shellfish to swim in rather jerky movements through the sea.
- **In fossils** and empty modern shells, the point at which the adductor muscle joined the inside of a valve can be seen as a small, rounded indentation. This is the muscle scar.
- ***Pecten*** has a triangular shell with a pointed umbo. The valves are flat and strengthened with ribs.

▼ *This mass of shells is from the early Jurassic. They are very like modern scallops and probably lived in a similar way, opening and closing their valves to swim.*

Fossil oysters

◄ *The wavy structure on this oyster shell is the edge of its fleshy body. Oysters have to open their shells so that they can feed.*

- **From the Mesozoic Era** to Recent times, oysters have been common marine shellfish.

- **Some fossil oysters** are very similar to those that live today, but others developed rather different shell shapes.

- **Unlike most bivalve mollusks,** oysters have valves that are not mirror images of each other. One valve is generally larger than the other.

- **Oysters cannot move freely** and they live on the seabed. They have a number of features that help them survive in shallow, turbulent water.

- **Usually,** an oyster has very thick, heavy valves. These are adapted to being washed around by currents and tides without being damaged.

- **The adductor muscle** is large and strong to hold the valves together when the shell is moved about by the sea.

- **As is typical of oysters,** *Gryphaea* had valves that are very different from each other. One valve was large and heavy, the other was thinner and smaller.

106

- **The larger valve** was hooked at one end and made of many layers of calcite.

- **This structure** probably allowed *Gryphaea* to lie on the seabed, with the heavy valve underneath. If disturbed by water currents, it would come to rest in this position again.

...FASCINATING FACT...
Because of its curved shape, *Gryphaea* is sometimes
called the "devil's toenail."

▶ Gryphaea *is a common fossil oyster from the Jurassic Period.*

Cenozoic bivalves

- **Many of the marine** bivalve mollusks that live today evolved during the Cenozoic Era.

- **Most of the shells** found on the beach are bivalve mollusks. Often, the more delicate ones are broken, but some, especially those adapted to live on the seabed, may be washed up undamaged.

- **During fossilization**, especially in shallow water where coarse sediment like sand is deposited, the strongest shells stand the best chance of being preserved.

- *Venericardia*, a type of clam, occurs in Paleocene and Eocene strata.

- **This bivalve lived** just below the surface of the mud or sand on the seabed, in a very shallow burrow.

- **It had a massive shell**, with strong ribs running across it to help withstand being disturbed and rolled around by sea currents.

- **The wide part** of the shell was in the upper part of the burrow very near the sediment surface, so that it could feed from the water.

- *Arctica*, a living clam, is similar to *Venericardia*. It has a strong shell adapted to shallow conditions, and lives in a shallow burrow.

- **Although *Arctica*** still survives today, it is also found fossilized in Eocene strata.

- **These two bivalves** rarely occur on their own as fossils. Usually, the strata in which they are found contains many other bivalves, gastropods, and fish teeth.

◀ *Arctica is a thick-shelled bivalve found in rocks from the Pliocene Epoch. It still lives today on the continental shelf, burrowing into sand and mud.*

109

Burrowing bivalves

- **Because they are protected** in their burrows, bivalves that tunnel into the seabed often have delicate shells.

- **Modern-day bivalves**, such as *Mya*, clams, and razor shells, show typical features of burrowing bivalves.

- **Fossils of *Pholadomya*** are commonly found in strata of Jurassic age.

- **The shell of this bivalve**, and that of other burrowers, is often lengthened. The posterior end (the one furthest away from the beak or umbo) is stretched.

- **The modern razor shell**, *Solen*, is a good example of the lengthened shell. In this bivalve, the shell is virtually a long, flattened tube.

- ***Pholadomya* is sometimes found** fossilized in its burrow, positioned vertically in the strata with the umbo downward.

- **As they are confined** in a burrow, these bivalves cannot open and close their valves to feed. The upper end of the shell, the posterior end, is always slightly open. This opening is called the gape.

- **Two fleshy tubes** called siphons stick out of the open end of the shell above the seabed. One sucks water and food in, the other blows water and waste out.

- **In fossils**, or shells washed up on the shore, there is often a thin line inside the shell. This is called the pallial line and marks where the edge of the animal's body joined the shell.

- **Burrowers have a deep kink** in the pallial line where the long siphons stuck out.

◀ *Modern razor shells burrow very rapidly into sand or mud on the seabed. This razor shell has its fleshy "foot" extending outside the shell.*

Freshwater bivalves

- **Many bivalves have adapted** to living in freshwater. About one-fifth of bivalves living today are found in lakes and rivers.

- **In some cases** where they are geographically isolated from other similar bivalves, new types have evolved.

- **Bivalves that live in freshwater** are different from their marine relatives.

- **Freshwater does not hold** as many shell-making chemicals as seawater does, so freshwater bivalves tend to have thinner, more delicate shells than marine ones.

- **Many different freshwater** bivalves are found fossilized in rocks of Carboniferous age.

- **During the later part** of the Carboniferous Period, much of Europe and North America was covered with river systems and deltas. Bivalve mollusks flourished in the streams and lakes on the deltas.

- ***Carbonicola*** is a typical inhabitant of Carboniferous waters. It is found fossilized in strata associated with coal beds.

- **This small bivalve** burrowed into the soft mud of streambeds.

- **Many years ago**, coal miners referred to the layers containing *Carbonicola* and other nonmarine bivalves as "mussel bands."

- **Most bivalves are not** much use for the relative dating of rock strata. However, the bivalves that lived in the Carboniferous rivers and swamps can help to link rocks geographically from place to place.

▲ *This thin-shelled bivalve lived in streams during the Carboniferous Period.*

113

Fossil gastropods

▲ Straparollus *moved slowly around the seabed,*
feeding. This specimen is from Carboniferous strata.

- **Some gastropods**, such as snails and limpets, have shells. Others, such as slugs, have no external shells.

- **Gastropods have evolved** since the Cambrian Period, which is when they first appear as fossils.

- **Fossil gastropods are not as common** as fossil bivalves and cephalopods.

- **There are probably more** gastropods alive today than at any time in the past.

- **Gastropods have adapted** to many habitats. Some live in the sea, both crawling on the seabed and floating as plankton. They are also common on dryland.

- *Poleumita* is a typical sea snail from Silurian marine strata.

- **This gastropod occurs** in limestones deposited in shallow water, including those formed on reefs.

- *Poleumita* **has a shell** that coils in a low spiral. There are ridges and small spines on the shell.

- *Straparollus* lived from the Silurian to Permian Periods. It had a fairly smooth shell and lived in shallow seas.

- **Gastropods**, such as these, are often found fossilized with many other mollusks, brachiopods, and corals. This shows that the habitat on the Paleozoic seabed was favorable to life.

Cenozoic sea snails

- **During the Cenozoic Era**, gastropods began to develop different groups that still live today.

- **Fossil gastropods** often have their original shell intact, showing as much detail as a modern shell found on the beach.

- **Though fossils of *Turritella*** first occurred in rocks of Cretaceous age, it evolved into a number of species during the Cenozoic Era.

- ***Turritella***, also known as towershell or turretshell, has a long, narrow shell with screwlike coiling. The fossil species are closely related to modern tower screw shells.

- **The coils of the shell** are called whorls. *Turritella* has a groove between each whorl.

- **The only details** on the shell are faint growth lines, which mark an earlier position of the shell opening.

- **Like many gastropods**, *Turritella* lived in shallow seas, and is found fossilized with other mollusks, corals, and crustaceans.

- **Masses of *Turritella* shells** sometimes appear together, and make up a high percentage of the rock.

- **Modern species** of *Turritella* usually burrow into the mud and silt on the seabed. The sharp end of the shell points downward and the opening is near the surface of the seabed.

- **It is probable that** fossil gastropods lived in a similar way. For them to be fossilized in large numbers, they must have been disturbed by sea currents and the shells washed together.

▶ *This mass of perfectly preserved* Turritella *shells is from Eocene strata in France.*

116

Predatory sea snails

- **During the Cretaceous Period**, gastropod mollusks were not as common as other groups, but in the Cenozoic Era they evolved rapidly.

- **Marine gastropods developed** many ways of feeding. Some became active predators.

- **Almost half the number** of fossilized gastropods found in rocks of Eocene age were predators.

- **These sea snails were not** very big, and many of them had sophisticated ways of killing and eating their prey.

- **Almost anything** living on the seabed would have been attacked by these snails. Sea urchins, mollusks, and worms were all eaten. Some species even caught live fish.

- *Conus*, the cone shell, was a typical predatory gastropod from the Eocene Epoch.

- **This small sea snail** had a very ornate shell, crossed by sharp ridges and lines. It is often fossilized in large masses.

- **Gastropods have a radula**, which is used for feeding. The radula is a sharp "tongue" that is used to attack prey or rasp off plant material.

- *Conus* **is found fossilized** with many other mollusks, fish teeth, echinoids, and corals.

...FASCINATING FACT...

Conus has a highly advanced radula that was like a thin harpoon. This was stuck into prey and then venom injected through a groove in the radula.

◄ *This modern cone shell shoots its poisonous radula into a whelk's shell. The venom is very powerful and quickly paralyzes the prey.*

Cephalopods

▲ *These cephalopods (Orthoceras) are from Ordovician rocks. They are straight-shelled nautiloids, and the buoyancy chambers can be seen where the shell has broken off.*

- **This class of mollusks** contains some of the most advanced invertebrates to have ever evolved.

- **The pearly nautilus**, octopus, squid, and cuttlefish are all cephalopods, as well as many extinct groups, such as ammonites and belemnites.

- **Modern cephalopods** have a highly developed nervous system and good eyesight.

- **All these creatures** live in the sea and most are capable of free movement, often by jet propulsion.

- **As well as squirting water** for propulsion, many cephalopods can emit a cloud of dark, inky liquid, behind which they can hide from predators.

- **Both the external** and internal shells of cephalopods are common as fossils.

- ***Orthoceras*** is an early, straight-shelled nautilus from lower Paleozoic strata. The shell, like that of many cephalopods, is divided into chambers, with the animal living in the largest one at the open end of the shell.

- **Some species of *Orthoceras*** grew to several feet in length, although most were only an inch or so long.

- **In some areas**, such as the limestone at Maquokota in Illinois, large numbers of *Orthoceras* are found fossilized together.

- **Specimens of *Orthoceras*** limestone containing these fossils are cut and polished for ornamental use.

▼ *The modern octopus is a free-swimming mollusk that lacks an outer shell. It is a very advanced animal with a complex nervous system and good eyesight.*

Devonian and Carboniferous cephalopods

- **In the upper Paleozoic Era**, especially during the Devonian and Carboniferous Periods, cephalopods evolved with coiled external shells.

- **The coiled shell** had many chambers. At the wide end of the shell was the body chamber in which the squidlike animal lived.

- **Many smaller buoyancy** chambers extended back from the body chamber to the tightly coiled center of the shell.

- **These chambers may have** been crushed on bedding planes during fossilization. However, in many cases they are preserved and infilled with crystals of minerals, such as calcite.

- **Some cephalopod shells** are similar to a coil of rope, with all the coils (whorls) easily seen. This is called evolute coiling.

- **Shells where the whorls** overlap a great deal are said to have involute coiling.

- **The goniatites are a group** of cephalopods that lived in the Devonian and Carboniferous seas.

Suture line

- **Goniatites** may have been the ancestors of the Mesozoic ammonites and generally had involute shells.

- **The suture lines** have a zigzag pattern and mark where the walls of the internal buoyancy chambers meet the outer shell.

- **The common**, free-swimming goniatites are used as zone fossils for marine strata of Devonian and Carboniferous age.

◀ *Goniatites are small cephalopods. The zigzag suture pattern is clearly seen in this example from the Carboniferous Period.*

123

Modern and Jurassic nautilus

- **The pearly nautilus,** which today lives in the southwestern Pacific Ocean mainly around Australia and Indonesia, is regarded as a "living fossil."

- **Fossils of similar species** of nautilus occur in rocks dating back to the early Mesozoic.

- **The nautilus** has a broad shell with involute coiling. The inner whorls are largely hidden by the large outermost whorl.

- *Cenoceras* was a Jurassic nautilus with many similar features to the modern pearly nautilus.

- **The suture lines on a nautilus** shell are gently curved, not zigzagged as in the goniatites, or complex as in the ammonites.

- **Like many shelled cephalopods,** the nautilus has a large body chamber. The squidlike animal has numerous tentacles, eyes, and a funnel for squirting water provides jet propulsion.

- **The smaller buoyancy chambers** are linked through their centers by a thin tube—the siphuncle. This allows the density of fluid and gas in the chambers to be regulated. The animal can then control its depth in the sea.

◀ Cenoceras *had a large body chamber, and the inner coils of the shell are covered by the large outermost coil.*

- **The nautilus has many** biological differences from the extinct ammonites. However, its shell is similar, and may give a good insight into how ammonites lived.

- **Because fossilized nautilus** shells span such a long period of time, they are little use as zone fossils.

- **Nautilus shells are found** washed ashore in east Africa and Madagascar, many hundreds of miles from where they live. Shells of dead ammonites could probably have drifted across the Mesozoic sea, thus enhancing their use as zone fossils.

▲ *The modern nautilus lives in the western Pacific Ocean, especially around Australia. It has good eyesight and moves by squirting out a jet of water.*

Ammonites

- **During the Jurassic** and Cretaceous Periods, ammonites evolved into a great variety of forms.

- **Ammonites were marine** creatures and many could move freely in the water, although some of the largest may have browsed on the seabed.

- **The ammonite shell** is similar to the nautilus shell, but there are some very important differences.

- **The spiral coiling** of the ammonite shell does not usually extend upward. It is coiled in a flat plane with both sides of the shell depressed in the center.

- **An ammonite shell** has a large body chamber at the shell opening. This chamber reaches back for about half a whorl. Usually, the animal lived with the body chamber at the lowest point, and the rest of the shell above.

- **A thin tube**, called the siphuncle, links the smaller buoyancy chambers. This runs along the outside of each whorl, not in the center as in the nautilus.

- **The buoyancy chambers** are separated from each other by walls called septa. Where these reach the shell, they become very complex. If some of the outer shell is worn away or removed, these complex patterns are revealed as suture lines.

- **Ammonite shells can be distinguished** from nautilus and goniatite shells by their wavy, frilly or lobed suture lines.

- *Psiloceras* is one of the first ammonites to appear in rocks of Jurassic age. As ammonites are used as zone fossils, it marks the base of the Jurassic Period.

- **This ammonite has a shell coiled** midway between involute and evolute, and only faint ridges running across the whorls.

Whorl

Frilly suture lines

Body chamber

▶ *It is unusual to find uncrushed specimens of Psiloceras. These examples are from a boulder washed up on the shore of North Yorkshire, UK.*

Ammonite variety and movement

◀ *This reconstruction shows the ammonite Lytoceras swimming in the warm Jurassic ocean. Ammonites had far fewer tentacles than the nautilus.*

- **Fossil ammonite shells** show a vast range of different shapes, sizes, and structures. The movement of different species may have depended on their shape.
- **Some ammonites were big** and round, others were thin and disk-shaped. Some had shells that were quite small, others very large.
- **The outer surface** of a fossil ammonite shell may be covered with ridges (ribs), spines, and knobs.
- **Exactly what function** these features had is unknown. Ribs may have added strength to the shell, and spines may have helped protect against predators.
- **For an animal that was able** to swim, various features of the shell could have kept the ammonite in the correct position and helped with streamlining.
- **Scientists have studied** how the nautilus moves in order to try and suggest the swimming ability of ammonites.
- **The nautilus** can move both slowly and in rapid bursts by using the muscles in its large body cavity, and by squirting water from its funnel.
- **Ammonites had a very different** body chamber from that of the nautilus. In the ammonite shell, the part occupied by the animal's body was generally narrow and tube-shaped, although some did have wide body chambers. The nautilus has a wide, expanded body chamber.
- **It is thought that** most ammonites were poor swimmers, especially when compared with modern squids.
- **By altering the fluids and gas** in the buoyancy chambers, ammonites could regulate their density, and were able to change their depth in the water.

Ammonite suture lines

- **One of the most striking features** of fossil ammonites is the pattern of complex lines that can often be seen running across the shell. These are called suture lines.

- **The suture lines** do not occur on the outside of the shell, and must not be confused with the ribs or other external markings.

- **Suture lines are on the inner surface** of the shell. Only slightly worn shells, or shells where some of the outermost material is broken off, show these complex lines.

- **Each suture line marks** where an internal division between two chambers joined the inner surface of the shell.

- **This join was very complicated**, as shown by the pattern of the suture lines.

- **Ammonite fossils often break**. A small fossil may be only the inner whorls of a large ammonite—the body chamber and large outer whorls having been destroyed.

▲ *When polished, and the outer layer of shell removed from this* Eparietites, *the intricate suture lines can be clearly seen.*

◀ Baculites *is an uncoiled ammonite from Cretaceous rocks. The very complex suture lines are typical of this genus.*

● **It is easy to tell** if an ammonite specimen is complete by looking at the suture lines.

● **In a complete ammonite shell**, there are no suture lines for the first half whorl or so. This is where the undivided body chamber is. The suture lines only begin where the buoyancy chambers are.

● **Suture patterns vary greatly** between ammonites. All are very complicated. Some have rounded shapes, some spiky patterns, and others are very wavy.

● **Ammonites are frequently sold** as ornaments. Often these are highly polished and the outer shell removed, to show the amazing suture patterns.

Spiny ammonites

- **Many ammonites have sharp**, spiny structures on their shells. These frequently break off during or before fossilization.

- **It has been suggested** that sharp spines on the shell helped protect the ammonite from predators.

- **A few ammonite shells** have been discovered with the impressions of jaw marks on them. These may be from a marine reptile, such as a mosasaur.

- **The spines on ammonite shells** are generally very delicate and hollow. They would probably not be much use against a predator, certainly not one the size of a mosasaur.

- **Another theory is** that spines and other structures on the outside of the shell may help with camouflage. The spines break up the shape of the ammonite shell, especially in deeper water, where light penetration is low.

- *Liparoceras* is an ammonite commonly found in rocks of Lower Jurassic age. In life, it had sharp spines on its shell. These are usually broken off in fossils with only their stumps remaining.

- **On the shell of *Liparoceras*,** the rows of knobs where the spines were can be easily seen. There are also wide ribs running across the shell.

- **As with many ammonites**, the ribs on the shell of *Liparoceras* divide and become more numerous as they run across the back of the shell.

- **Where *Liparoceras* is found**, there is often a smaller ammonite called *Aegoceras*. This looks exactly like the inner whorls of *Liparoceras*.

- **Some paleontologists believe** that these two ammonites are males and females of the same species.

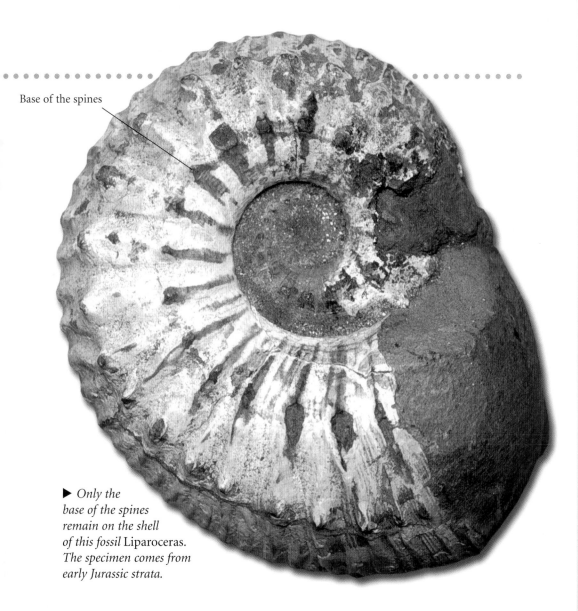

Base of the spines

▶ *Only the
base of the spines
remain on the shell
of this fossil* Liparoceras.
*The specimen comes from
early Jurassic strata.*

Ammonite names

- **Fossils are named** for many reasons. Often the fossil's name is the Latin version of the name of the person who first found it.

- **Sometimes**, a fossil's name is derived from the place where it was first found, or after a special feature it has. The scientific name may tell us something about the fossil's shape.

- **The Jurassic rocks** in North Yorkshire, UK, can be easily observed at the coast. These strata have been studied for hundreds of years.

- **Around the town of Whitby** in North Yorkshire, UK, the Lower Jurassic rocks form high cliffs below St Hilda's Abbey. These rocks were originally layers of mud on the Jurassic seabed.

- **Many creatures lived in** this Jurassic sea. Fossils of mollusks, fish, and reptiles show that the Jurassic sea was full of life.

- **The ammonite** *Hildoceras* is named after St Hilda, who founded the abbey on the cliff tops at Whitby.

- **Ammonites are associated** with Whitby to such an extent that the town's coat of arms contains three of them.

- **Famous geologists** of the 19th century learned a lot from the strata on the Yorkshire coast. These include William Smith (1769–1839), who pioneered the use of fossils for correlating strata from one place to another.

- **Further south** on this coast in the town of Scarborough, Smith designed the Rotunda Museum in such a way that fossils could be displayed depending on distribution, and the age of the sedimentary rock they were found in.

...FASCINATING FACT...
It was once believed that ammonites were snakes that had been turned to stone by St Hilda. Local craftsmen used to carve snakes' heads on ammonites to perpetuate the myth.

◀ *A head has been carved on this ammonite shell to illustrate the myth that ammonites are fossilized snakes.*

Giant ammonites

- **Ammonite shells vary** greatly in size. The majority are a few inches in diameter, some are much larger.

- **In order to study** ammonite shells and determine the average size of different species, certain rules have to be followed.

- **Before measuring the size** of a fossilized ammonite shell, it is important to make sure it is complete. This is done by examining the shell carefully and looking for the suture lines.

- **A lack of suture lines** near the shell opening shows that the body chamber is present. The shell will be complete if this is the case.

- **Paleontologists** also have certain ways of telling if an ammonite is a small juvenile.

- **Mature shells often have** widened shell openings and the last few sutures crowd together.

- **One of the largest ammonites** is aptly named *Titanites*. It could grow to about 3 ft in diameter.

- ***Titanites*** occurs in late Jurassic rocks. It is loosely coiled and has strong ribs crossing the shell.

- **An even larger ammonite** is *Parapuzosia*, from late Cretaceous strata, which grew to about 8 ft in diameter.

- **It is probable that** such large ammonites lived near, or on, the seabed rather than swimming freely.

▶ *This specimen of* Titanites *is about 3 ft in diameter. It is on display in the Geology Department at the University of Keele in Staffordshire, UK.*

Titanites titan S.S. BUCKMAN 1921
UPPER JURASSIC PORTLANDIAN STAGE·
DORSET, ENGLAND.
"TYPE AMMONITES" VOL III. PLATE CCXXXI
PRESENTED BY H.M. GEOLOGICAL SURVEY

Uncoiled ammonites

- **The classic ammonite shell** is coiled in a flat spiral. Some shells have a large body chamber that overlaps the smaller, inner whorls.

- **During ammonite evolution**, many different shells appeared that don't look like typical ammonites.

▲ *This uncoiled* Spiroceras *shell has many ammonite features. There are ribs, and the shell tapers at one end.*

- **At many times** during the Jurassic and Cretaceous periods, some ammonite species developed uncoiled shells.

- **Toward the end** of their evolution in the late Cretaceous Period, uncoiling was common. Other strange shapes also appeared at this time.

- **One of the strangest** of these is *Didymoceras,* which occurs in the Cretaceous rocks of Colorado.

- **This ammonite** is the corkscrew shape of a ram's horn, coiled in a very open spiral.

- **Many uncoiled ammonites** have a more U-shaped structure, like *Hamites* from the Cretaceous Period.

- *Spiroceras* is from Jurassic strata. By uncoiling, it has lost the classic ammonite symmetry.

- *Spiroceras* **retains some** ammonite features, such as the thick ribs that run across the shell.

- **Uncoiled ammonites** were probably poorer swimmers than their coiled relatives. An uncoiled shell would not be as stable, and these ammonites may have moved slowly along the seabed, feeding.

Ammonites as zone fossils

▲ *This specimen of* Asteroceras *is complete. Sutures are absent from the last part of the shell because this is the undivided body chamber.*

- **Zone fossils help** paleontologists to put strata into sequences. They also allow strata to be linked, or correlated from place to place.

- **For a fossil group** to be chosen for this work, it must have certain features. Ammonites are probably the best zone fossils as they have virtually all the requirements.

- **A relative time zone** should be as short as possible. This allows very precise dating of rocks. It is not much use having a time zone tens of millions of years long. Far too many rocks form in such a huge expanse of time, and correlating them would be too difficult.

- **The ammonite species** chosen as zone fossils represent small parts of geological time.

- **Ammonites evolved** very rapidly into many species. Each species lived for a relatively short time before becoming extinct.

- **Because ammonites lived in the sea** and could move about, certain species are found in many different regions. They are useful in correlating strata from place to place.

- **Shells of dead ammonites** could drift on ocean currents as modern nautilus shells do, and be carried to distant places.

- **A zone fossil** should be easily fossilized. A jellyfish may have all the attributes required for correlating rocks, but it is rarely found as a fossil. Ammonite shells are easily preserved.

- **It is important** for a zone fossil to be common. Field geologists need to be able to find them to do their work. Ammonites are numerous in Jurassic and Cretaceous rocks, and these periods are zoned by ammonites.

- **Because of their varied structures,** it is easy to tell one zone ammonite from another, making that part of the geological time scale easy to work out.

◀ *Dozens of* Asteroceras *species are known from many parts of the world during the Jurassic Period.* Asteroceras *means "star horn."*

141

Cretaceous ammonites

- **During the Cretaceous Period**, ammonites flourished and many new shell shapes evolved.

- **Some Cretaceous ammonites** were uncoiled with straight shells. Others were curved, and almost U-shaped.

- *Baculites*, a straight Cretaceous ammonite, is well-known for its remarkable pattern of suture lines.

- **This ammonite is common** in Cretaceous rocks in South Dakota. It grew to a great size, reaching up to 6 ft in length.

- *Scaphites* is a partly uncoiled ammonite from the Cretaceous Period.

- **The body chamber** of *Scaphites* is large and uncoiled. An ammonite with this structure was probably not adapted to swimming. It more likely lived on or near the seabed, with the shell opening slightly upward.

- *Douvilleiceras* is a Cretaceous ammonite with the usual ammonite coiling. It had rows of large knobs running around the shell.

- **This ammonite is widespread** and common in Cretaceous rocks, and is used as a zone fossil for this period.

- *Mantelliceras* lived in the Cretaceous sea, on the bed that chalk was being deposited on. It had strong ribs running across its shell.

- **At the end of the Cretaceous Period**, ammonites became extinct. The exact reasons for this are unknown, although they had been declining in numbers of genera for some time. At the same time, many other groups of animals, both on land (for example, the dinosaurs) and in the sea (75 percent of marine plankton) died out.

▲ *This dusty, white specimen of* Douvilleiceras *is found in upper Cretaceous rocks where chalk is the dominant rock.*

Ammonites with beaks

- **Certain ammonites have** a strange beaklike structure on the front of the shell. This is called a lappet.

- *Kosmoceras* is a small ammonite well-known for this lappet structure.

- **This ammonite is found** in rocks formed during the middle part of Jurassic time. It has ribs running across the shell and spines along the shell margin.

- **In the clay strata** where these ammonite shells occur, they are usually crushed flat, but original shell material is often preserved.

- **Much larger forms** of *Kosmoceras* are found fossilized with the smaller shells.

- **Paleontologists studying both** these ammonites discovered that changes in their shells occurred at the same time. When a new feature developed on the small shell, the same feature appeared on the larger shell.

- **This side-by-side evolution** of two ammonites, one larger than the other, has been found to occur with other species.

Lappet

▲ *This specimen of* Kosmoceras *with its lappet intact, is from Middle Jurassic strata.*

• **Paleontologists have analyzed** hundreds of specimens of *Kosmoceras* in order to try and understand the evolution of the two size forms of the ammonite.

• **It is believed that** the large and small *Kosmoceras* may be males and females of the same species. This would explain their simultaneous evolutionary changes. The sexes of many modern cephalopods have a distinct size difference.

• **The exact purpose** of the lappet on the smaller fossil shell is unknown. Some paleontologists suggest that the small shell was the male and the lappet was a display device.

Fossil squids

- **Squids are cephalopods** with an internal shell. These shells are common fossils in Mesozoic sedimentary strata.

- **The fossilized internal shells** of cephalopods are similar to squid and are called belemnites.

- **Belemnites first appear** as fossils in rocks of the Carboniferous Period, and became extinct just before or early in the Cenozoic Era.

- **The long, bullet-shaped** fossil, varying in length from 0.5–6 in or more, is called the guard.

- **As well as the narrow**, tapering part of the shell, there is a much wider, chambered part, called the phragmocone. This fits into the wider end of the guard.

- **Belemnites are solid objects**, made of layers of calcite, so they usually retain their three-dimensional shape when fossilized.

Guard

- **Where masses of belemnites occur** on rock surfaces, they are often all parallel to each other. This suggests that they were moved by seabed currents.

- **The belemnite's soft body** was like that of a typical squid with tentacles, eyes, and a funnel for squirting water or ink.

- **Belemnites were probably** free-swimming, rather like modern squids, although modern squids have not evolved directly from them.

- **Fossil belemnite ink sacs** have been found in Jurassic strata. In the 19th century, paleontologists reconstituted the "ink" and used it for writing.

▼ *This is an unusual belemnite fossil, as the crushed phragmocone is preserved with the narrow, tapering guard.*

Phragmocone

Tusk shells

- **Tusk shells are alive today** and are mollusks that belong to a class called the scaphopods. The earliest tusk shells occur in rocks of Ordovician age.

- **A scaphopod shell** is a thin tube that is open at each end.

- **The name "tusk shell"** describes the way many of these shells curve and taper like an elephant's tusk.

- **Modern** tusk shells give many clues as to how prehistoric species may have lived. Today, tusk shells live in shallow seas, mainly on the continental shelf.

- **The animal burrows** at a shallow angle into the seabed sediment and pulls itself down using a muscular foot.

- **Its head is in the deepest part** of the burrow. The narrow end of the shell, containing the anus, projects a short distance above the seabed.

- **Using specially adapted tentacles**, the tusk shell feeds on minute organisms living in the mud on the seabed.

▲ *These tusk shells,* Dentalium, *are from strata of the Miocene Epoch in Tuscany, Italy.*

- **Fossil tusk shells** are often well preserved. When the creature died, the hollow shell could easily fill with mud. This would prevent it from being crushed.

- *Dentalium* is found in rocks ranging in age from Cretaceous to Recent. It has changed little in many tens of million of years.

...FASCINATING FACT...
Fossil tusk shells have been used by people through the ages for necklaces, nose piercings, and as currency for trading.

Vertebrate fossils

- **Vertebrates are creatures** that have internal skeletons usually made of bone or cartilage and incorporating a backbone. They include fish, amphibians, reptiles, birds, and mammals.

- **For a number of reasons**, the fossils of vertebrates are not as common as those of shellfish, arthropods, corals, and other invertebrates.

▼ Cephalaspis *was an early fossil fish from* *Devonian strata. Many early fish, including* Cephalaspis, *lived in freshwater lakes.*

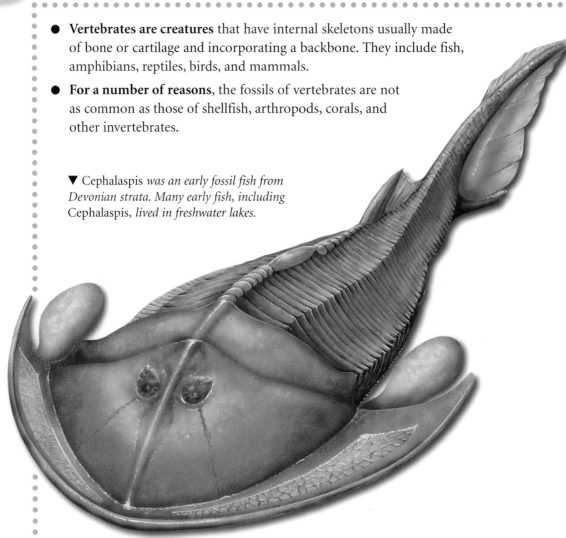

- **Creatures with backbones** evolved much later than most invertebrates. While trilobites and brachiopods were being fossilized in the Cambrian and Ordovician periods, there were no vertebrates.

- **Many vertebrates** live on land. Here, erosion and weathering take place rather than the deposition of sediment, such as mud and sand.

- **The remains** of a vertebrate will probably decay and be broken up rather than be covered with fossilizing sediment.

- **Many vertebrate fossils** are broken and scattered bones rather than whole skeletons.

- **However**, there are many excellent cases of masses of vertebrates, including dinosaurs being fossilized in deposits formed on land, such as those in China and North America.

- **Fish were the first** vertebrates to evolve. Because they live in water, many of them are fossilized.

- *Cephalaspis* was a primitive fish from the Devonian Period.

- **The large head shield** of the *Cephalaspis* had eye sockets on the top, and the mouth was underneath. Like the modern lamprey, it had a sucker-like mouth rather than true jaws.

Early fossil fish

- **Vertebrate evolution** took a great step forward when fish began to survive, even for just a short period of time, out of the water.

- **During the Devonian Period**, a vast continent existed comprising what is now Greenland, North America, and northwest Europe.

- **The Devonian continent** was dry and mountainous, but there were great inland freshwater lakes teeming with fish.

- **The remains of many** of these fish are preserved in the muddy sandstone that formed on the lakebeds.

▶ Dipterus *is a fossil fish that lived in freshwater lakes during the Devonian Period. It could have possibly survived out of water for some time.*

- **Fish living in** freshwater ponds and lakes are often fossilized in large numbers. If part of the lake system dries up, many fish die at the same time.

- **Fish scales** are very durable and are easily preserved as fossils.

- *Dipterus* was one of the many different fish that lived in Devonian lakes.

- *Dipterus* **had a short body** with a large head.

- **Its fins had bony** strengthening, which may have been able to support the weight of its body.

- *Dipterus* **was very similar** to modern lungfish.

Armored fish

- *Bothriolepis* comes from the renowned fossil site of Miguasha near Scaumenac Bay in Canada.

- **Fossils were first discovered** at this now-famous site in the mid-19th century.

- **The rocks there contain** thousands of exceptionally well-preserved fossils of fish and other organisms.

- **These remarkable numbers** of fine fossils have attracted both professional and amateur collectors.

- **In order to prevent** fossil collectors from ravaging the site, the Miguasha National Park was set up in 1985. In 1999, it became a world heritage site. New finds are kept in the museum there.

- **Early fish were often covered** with large scales and protective armor.

- *Bothriolepis* had a large head shield, which is the only part usually fossilized.

● **The head shield** was heavily armored and covered with rough, bony plates.

● **Extending from each side** of the head were two long, narrow, finlike projections.

● **Paleontologists** have cut many of the well-preserved fossils from Miguasha into sections. They discovered internal details, such as two large sacs leading from the pharynx (throat). These may have been lungs.

◄ *Only the heavily armored head shield and armlike projections of this* Bothriolepis *have been preserved.*

155

The Green River fish

◄ Knightia *is one of many fish species preserved in the famous Green River strata.*

- **Exceptional numbers** of fossil fish are preserved in the Green River strata of Wyoming, Colorado, and Utah.

- **These rocks are limestones** formed in the Eocene Epoch.

- **It seems that during** Eocene times, a number of large lakes existed in the Green River region.

- **Fossil pollen** found in the strata shows that dense vegetation grew around the lakes.

- **Many different genera** of fish lived in the Green River area. Fossils of *Knightia, Diplomystus, Gosuitichthys,* and *Priscacara* are all common.

- **Small rock slabs** covered with some of these fish are sold in fossil shops.

- **The climate** in the Green River region during the Eocene Epoch, was probably warm with definite seasons.

- **In the drier season**, the lakes became smaller, and many fish died and became fossilized as the lakes dried up.

- ***Gosuitichthys*** is in many ways a modern fish, with its backbone near the dorsal surface and masses of ribs supporting the body.

- **Many of the Green River** fossil fish are perfectly preserved, but some are in small pieces. This may be because they exploded during decomposition.

◄ *When water in one of the Green River lakes dried up, this mass of* Gosuitichthys *died and was covered with mud.*

Fossil fish teeth

▼ *This fossil tooth is from an extinct type of* Carcharodon, *which grew far larger than today's great white shark.*

● **Fish teeth** are made of very durable material, and are often the only part of the creature that becomes fossilized.

● **In some strata** formed during the Cenozoic Era, there are large numbers of fossil fish teeth, especially those of sharks.

● **Many sharks do not have** true bony skeletons, and their teeth are all that remain as fossils.

● **By comparing fossil** fish teeth with those of modern fish, it is usually possible to say what the ancient fish were like.

● **Two fossil sharks** that are known mainly from their teeth are *Lamna* and *Odontaspis*.

● **These sharks were** medium-sized predators that grew to about 12 ft in length.

● **The genus** *Carcharodon* is one of the best-known fossil sharks. It also includes today's great white shark.

- **Fossil *Carcharodon*** teeth sometimes called *Carcharodon megalodon*, can be as long as 6 in and occur in Cenozoic strata.

- **From the large size** of the teeth, it seems that this shark may have grown over 50 ft in length.

- **The teeth of *Carcharodon*** are triangular in shape with rows of sharp serrations along their edges.

▲ *The prehistoric shark,*
Hybodus, *was a fierce predator,*
and had many rows of triangular,
backward-facing teeth.

159

Early amphibians

▼ *This fossil temnospondyl (primitive amphibian) is from Odenheim, Germany. Only an outline of its body remains, with black carbon traces of the skeleton. It resembles today's newts and salamanders.*

- **The earliest fossil amphibians** are found in rocks of Devonian age.

- **The first amphibians** probably evolved from fish, such as lungfish, which are similar to *Dipterus*.

- **Modern amphibians** depend on water for survival. Most lay their eggs in water, and their young live in water before being able to breathe air and live on land.

- **Temnospondyls** are a group of early amphibians. Their fossils occur in Carboniferous and younger rocks.

- **With a bony skeleton** and limbs, temnospondyls share many features with modern amphibians.

160

- **Temnospondyls** had a flexible body, which was probably well-adapted to moving in damp habitats.
- **In West Lothian**, Scotland, UK, virtually complete temnospondyl skeletons have been found in rock of Carboniferous age.
- **The late** Carboniferous swamps were an ideal habitat for amphibians.
- **As well as temnospondyl** fossils, the Scottish late Carboniferous rocks contain fossils of scorpions, myriapods, and spiders. These are mainly land-dwelling creatures.

- **Reptiles** evolved from amphibians during the Carboniferous Period.

Mosasaurus

▼ *Mosasaurs were excellent swimmers that hunted for fish and other prey in Mesozoic seas.*

- **During the Mesozoic Era**, reptiles developed into many different types, some living on land and others in the sea.

- **The Mesozoic sea** teemed with life, and giant sea reptiles preyed on fish, mollusks, and other invertebrates.

- *Mosasaurus* was a very large marine reptile (about 50 ft long) that lived during the Cretaceous Period.

- **Often**, only its sharp teeth are fossilized. These are more than 2 in long. They curve slightly to a sharp point.

- *Mosasaurus* fossils have been found in North America and Northern Europe.

- **The body** of *Mosasaurus* was slender, and it used its powerful tail to propel itself through the water.

- **A study of *Mosasaurus*** skulls has shown that there are many similarities with those of monitor lizards, which live today.

- **Most mosasaurs** probably caught vertebrate prey, including fish. Some had teeth adapted for crushing.

- **The first *Mosasaurus*** remains were found in 1770 in the Netherlands. When first discovered, nobody knew what the giant fossil jaws were.

- **The name *Mosasaurus*** refers to the Meuse region in the Netherlands where the remains were found.

▶ *These vertebrae and ribs of a fossil mosasaur are from Cretaceous rocks in France.*

Pliosaurus and Plesiosaurus

- **The fossilized bones** of *Plesiosaurus* and *Pliosaurus* are not uncommon in Mesozoic strata.

- **The Lower Jurassic rocks** at Lyme Regis, Dorset, UK, have been a well-known fossil site since the early 19th century. Even today, fossil collectors scour the rocks exposed on the shore.

- **The first** *Plesiosaurus* was found at Lyme Regis by Mary Anning in 1821.

- *Plesiosaurus* grew to around 40 ft in length, and its most notable feature was its long neck.

- **The body of** *Plesiosaurus* was short and stout, with four large paddle-shaped limbs.

- *Plesiosaurus* had a small head, and its jaw was filled with many sharp teeth.

- **Using its long**, flexible neck, *Plesiosaurus* may have fed by slinging its head at prey.

- *Pliosaurus* was very similar to *Plesiosaurus*, but had a much shorter neck with a large head.

- *Pliosaurus* probably hunted live prey including reptiles, fish, and mollusks, such as ammonites.

In 1824, Mary Anning sold the first *Plesiosaurus* skeleton to the Duke of Buckingham for £100 ($200)—a huge sum in those days.

◄ *This short-necked pliosaur was an active hunter in the Jurassic seas.*

Ichthyosaurus

- **Fossils** of *Ichthyosaurus* have been known since the beginning of the 19th century.

- **These fossil** marine reptiles are found in rocks of Triassic, Jurassic, and Cretaceous age.

- ***Ichthyosaurus*** lacked the long neck of *Plesiosaurus*, and had a long, beaklike snout.

- **The mouth** was filled with conical, grooved teeth, designed for tearing prey apart.

▲ *This ichthyosaur's skeleton shows a strong spine that allowed the body to bend during movement in the water. The large eye sockets indicate good vision.*

166

- **The body of *Ichthyosaurus*** was streamlined, with a large, pointed dorsal fin and powerful front paddle fins. The rear pair of fins was much smaller.

- **The tail had bones** only in the lower part, and would have probably moved the animal upward as well as forward in the water.

- **Many remarkable** fossil ichthyosaurs have been found. Whole skeletons surrounded by a black impression of the body, including details of the paddles and tail, occur in Germany.

- **Fossils have proved** that *Ichthyosaurus* gave birth to live young. At least one adult skeleton has been found with a juvenile skeleton inside it.

- **Cephalopods**, including ammonites, had hooks on their tentacles. One *Ichthyosaurus* stomach contained the hooks from at least 1,600 cephalopods.

... FASCINATING FACT ...
An *Ichthyosaurus* that died giving birth has been fossilized, with the baby skeleton protruding from the birth canal.

Dinosaurs

▲ *A reconstruction of a Cretaceous scene.*

168

- **The dinosaurs** were a group of reptiles that evolved during the Mesozoic Era (248–65 million years ago). The name dinosaur means "terrible lizard."

- **All dinosaurs** lived on land. Some may have wandered into freshwater swamps but none lived in the sea.

- **Dinosaurs** are classified in a group of reptiles called the archosaurs.

- **Other archosaurs** include crocodiles and the extinct flying pterosaurs.

- **Dinosaurs** were a very varied and successful group. They lived for around 165 million years, before becoming extinct at the end of the Cretaceous Period.

- **Some dinosaurs**, such as *Diplodocus*, were enormous and slow moving. Others, like *Compsognathus*, were small and nimble.

- **Many dinosaurs** laid eggs, from which their young hatched. Dinosaur nests have been found, including those of *Protoceratops* in Mongolia.

KEY

1 *Edmontonia*
2 *Stegoceras*
3 *Triceratops*
4 *Avimimus*
5 *Lambeosaurus*
6 *Struthiomimus*
7 *Albertosaurus*
8 *Corythosaurus*
9 *Parasaurolophus*
10 *Euoplocephalus*
11 *Tyrannosaurus*

- **Dinosaurs** evolved to live in many habitats and to eat different food. *Allosaurus* was a predatory carnivore (meat eater) and *Stegosaurus* was a herbivore (plant eater).

- **There are many** theories about dinosaur extinction. It is probable that a giant meteorite hit the Earth in Mexico, this would have altered the climate and destroyed food chains.

- **Perhaps dinosaurs** are not extinct. If you see a pheasant, note how similar it is to one of the long-tailed, two-legged dinosaurs. Birds are thought to have evolved from dinosaurs, and may simply be modern, feathered versions of the prehistoric reptiles.

Stegosaurus

- *Stegosaurus* lived during the late Jurassic Period (160–145 million years ago).

- **This was** a relatively large dinosaur, with adults growing to about 30 ft in length, and possibly weighing up to 2 tons.

- **Fossils** of *Stegosaurus* come mainly from the western parts of North America, especially Wyoming, Utah, and Colorado. Relatives of *Stegosaurus* such as *Kentrosaurus* have been found fossilized in South East Africa and fossils of *Tujiangosaurus* have been found in East Asia.

- *Stegosaurus* was a thick-set dinosaur that walked on all four legs.

- **Along its back**, Stego*saurus* had a double row of large, relatively flat, bony plates.

- **The tail** of *Stegosaurus* was heavy and thick where it joined the body. It tapered rapidly to a point, and at the end it had four large bony spikes.

- **There are** a number of theories as to the function of the bony plates. They may have contained blood vessels, and so adjusted body temperature.

Brain cavity

Snout

▲ *This fossilized* Stegosaurus *skull shows the narrow snout and very small brain cavity.*

170

▼ Stegosaurus *had a tiny head in comparison to its body. Its brain was tiny too, indicating a lack of intelligence.*

- **The bony plates** could have been held flat against the body as a means of defense, and the tail spikes may have been used to swing at attackers.

- *Stegosaurus* had a very small head. The mouth had tiny serrated teeth. It is possible that food was broken down by stones in its stomach, which the animal swallowed, rather than by its teeth.

- *Stegosaurus* moved slowly, and fed on vegetation. It would probably have been preyed on by carnivores such as *Allosaurus*.

Triceratops

◄ *The horned beak of* Triceratops *was used for tearing food. The teeth, used for chewing, were well back in its cheeks.*

- *Triceratops* lived around 70 to 65 million years ago, during the late Cretaceous Period. It was one of the last dinosaurs.

- **The name *Triceratops* means "three-horned face."**

- **Most of the fossils** of *Triceratops* have been found in central North America, in Montana, North and South Dakota, and Wyoming. Fossils have also been found in Alberta and Saskatchewan in Canada.

- **This dinosaur** was stocky and thick-set. It grew to about 30 ft in length, and weighed about 5 tons.

- *Triceratops* is easily recognized by its large frilly head shield and three large, forward-facing horns.

- **The shield** around the neck probably helped to control body temperature, as it was supplied with blood vessels.

- **The horns** may have been for defense, or to help with feeding, by pulling tree branches down toward the mouth.

- **With its head down** and long, sharp horns pointing forward, *Triceratops* may have been able to fight off large predators.

- **Walking** on all four legs, it is thought that *Triceratops* lived in herds, wandering through the Cretaceous forests.

Like modern male deer, male *Triceratops* may have fought
each other with their horns to secure mates.

▼ *Complete skeletons, such as this one from North America, show where the muscles and
other soft tissues were attached, and allow accurate reconstructions of* Triceratops.

Compsognathus

▼ *The very delicate bone structure, teeth, and skull are very well preserved in this specimen of* Compsognathus.

- **Not all dinosaurs** were large. *Compsognathus* grew to only 5 ft in length. It probably weighed around 7 lb—about the same size as a pet cat.

- **Fossils of *Compsognathus*** have been discovered in France and Germany.

▼ Compsognathus *was a fierce predator of small prey, such as insects, lizards, and perhaps even newly hatched dinosaurs.*

- *Compsognathus* fossils from Germany occur in the same strata as those of the earliest bird, *Archaeopteryx*.

- *Compsognathus* lived during the late Jurassic Period, around 150 million years ago.

- **This dinosaur** was slender, with a very long, thin tail and a long neck.

- **The head** was large, and equipped with small, sharp teeth. The large eyes would have helped it to follow fast-moving prey.

- **With long**, thin legs, *Compsognathus* would have been able to run quickly in pursuit of prey, such as lizards.

- **This dinosaur** probably fed on smaller vertebrates and on invertebrates such as worms and insects, using its two sharp claws on each hand for gripping.

- *Compsognathus* lived around warm, salty lagoons, in a richly vegetated area. Limestone that formed in the lagoons contains some of the best-preserved fossils ever discovered.

...FASCINATING FACT...
Because the fossils of *Compsognathus* and *Archaeopteryx* are so similar, paleontologists originally mistook some *Archaeopteryx* fossils for those of *Compsognathus*.

Allosaurus

- **Allosaurus** was a fierce, predatory dinosaur that lived in late Jurassic times about 150 million years ago.

- **This dinosaur** grew to around 36 ft in length, and may have weighed up to 2–3 tons.

- **Allosaurus** stood on its large back limbs, and used its smaller front pair for grasping prey.

- **The fingers** on the front limbs each had long, sharp, backward-pointing claws.

- **The skull** was large but lightweight. The mouth was filled with curved, serrated teeth, ideal for tearing flesh.

- **The tail** was long and tapering. This would have balanced the weight of *Allosaurus'* neck and body as it stood upright.

- **Allosaurus** fossils have mainly been found in the USA. Some fossils also occur in southern Africa and a similar type in Victoria, Australia.

◀ *A fossilized* Allosaurus *claw. The large claws were used to grasp and tear at prey.* Allosaurus *probably ate herbivorous dinosaurs, including giant sauropods.*

▲ Allosaurus *had jaws that could bend slightly to allow them to open extremely wide. Together with its vicious front claws, this made* Allosaurus *a fearful predator.*

- **One of the most spectacular** collections of dinosaur bones ever found was a mass of over 60 *Allosaurus* skeletons. These were discovered at the Cleveland-Lloyd Dinosaur Quarry in Utah.

- **It has been suggested** that these 60 *Allosaurus* became trapped in a swamp as they attacked giant sauropods feeding there.

- **Herbivorous dinosaurs** were the main prey of *Allosaurus*. The large sauropod dinosaurs, such as *Diplodocus*, may have lived in herds for safety.

Iguanodon

◀ Iguanodon's "hands" were probably very good at grasping vegetation.

- **Iguanodon** was a large, herbivorous dinosaur that lived during the early part of the Cretaceous Period (135 million years ago).

- **This dinosaur** grew to around 33 ft long, and may have weighed 4 tons.

- **Iguanodon** walked on its strong hind legs, and may at times have also moved on all four limbs.

- **The front limbs** were designed for grasping, with long flexible "fingers."

- **Fossils** of *Iguanodon* have been found mainly in Europe, in Belgium, Germany, and Spain. The first was discovered in Sussex, UK, in the 1820s.

- **Iguanodon** was first described by Gideon Mantell, an English medical doctor and fossil collector, in 1825. His wife had earlier found the fossil teeth in a heap of stones by the road.

- **The fossil teeth** were very like those of a modern iguana. Mantell therefore named the dinosaur *Iguanodon*.

- **Iguanodon** fed on plant material, which it grasped using its hands. Its teeth, set in a beaklike snout, were for grinding vegetation.

...FASCINATING FACT...

On its "hand," *Iguanodon* had a large thumb-spike. Early paleontologists thought this was a horn that fitted on the creature's nose.

● **Over 30** complete *Iguanodon* skeletons were discovered in a coal mine in Belgium in 1878. It seems that a herd had become trapped in a ravine and had been preserved by sand and mud.

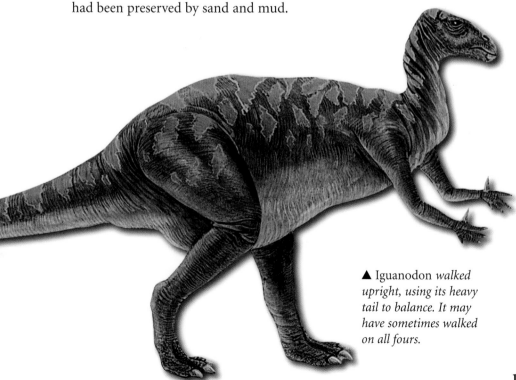

▲ Iguanodon *walked upright, using its heavy tail to balance. It may have sometimes walked on all fours.*

179

Saurolophus

- **Saurolophus** belongs to a group of dinosaurs classified as the hadrosaurs. They are sometimes called duck-billed dinosaurs.

- **Fossil hadrosaurs** occur mainly in North America, but some have been found in eastern Asia.

- **This group** of dinosaurs lived toward the end of the Cretaceous Period, about 80–70 million years ago.

- **Hadrosaurs** were large, upright-standing dinosaurs, which grew to around 40 ft in length.

- **The hind limbs** were strong, for walking, and the front limbs much smaller, for grasping plant material.

- **Plants** were chewed by the many rows of teeth in the animal's cheeks.

- **Hadrosaurs** had unusual skulls, with wide, elongated, beaklike snouts.

- **On the top** of the skull was a bony crest, which in some genera, such as *Parasaurolophus*, extended well beyond the back of the head.

- **Many suggestions** have been made by paleontologists for the function of the hadrosaur crest. It was linked to the nostrils by hollow passages, and may have been used for air storage, when the animal fed on underwater plants.

  - **The hadrosaur's bony crest** may have given it a very good sense of smell. This was important for a creature that was preyed on by carnivores.

◀ *The bony crest was the most distinctive feature of* Parasaurolopus. *Its exact function is not certain, but it was probably linked to the respiratory system, and may have been used to make sounds, such as honks and bellows, perhaps at breeding time.*

Tyrannosaurus

- **Tyrannosaurus** is one of the most famous dinosaurs. Its name has become synonymous with fierce predation.

- **This dinosaur** was one of the very last to evolve. It lived toward the end of the Cretaceous Period, around 70–65 million years ago.

- **Fossils** of *Tyrannosaurus* come from Canada (Alberta and Saskatchewan) and the USA (Wyoming, Montana, and Colorado).

- **The first** *Tyrannosaurus* **fossils** were discovered in 1902, and for many years only a few skeletons were known. In the last 40 years, many new finds have been made.

- **Tyrannosaurus** was a giant predator, growing to more than 40 ft in length and weighing as much as 6.5 tons.

- **This huge dinosaur** stood and walked on its massive hind legs. The weight of its body was balanced by its thick tail.

▲ *There is evidence that* Tyrannosaurus, *and certain other dinosaurs, may have had feather-like growths on their scaly skin.*

182

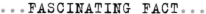

The front limbs of *Tyrannosaurus* were
very small—no longer than our arms.

- **It is thought** that *Tyrannosaurus* could run at
around 20 mph, especially when chasing prey.

- **The teeth** in its huge jaws were up to 7 in long.
They had serrations, which would help tear flesh.

- **The skull** had very strong muscles to provide
power to the jaws. It also had flexible areas,
which may have helped to cushion collisions
when attacking prey.

▼ *The skull of* Tyrannosaurus *was
flexible and lightweight. The large,
rear-facing teeth are well preserved
in this specimen.*

Deinonychus

- **Though small**, *Deinonychus* was one of the fiercest predators, equipped with vicious claws and teeth.

- ***Deinonychus*** lived during the middle of the Cretaceous Period, about 115–105 million years ago.

- **Fossils** of *Deinonychus* have been found in Montana and Wyoming.

- **This dinosaur** grew to about 10 ft in length and weighed 130 lb.

▶ *The skeleton of* Deinonychus *suggests that it was a fast-moving dinosaur, capable of leaping onto prey.*

- **The skeleton** of *Deinonychus* reveals that it was a very active dinosaur. It would have run rapidly, and could probably leap onto large dinosaurs as it attacked them.

- **The tail** was stiffened by bony tendons and strongly interlocking vertebrae.

- **The elongated head** contained rows of backward-facing, saw-edged teeth, and the hind feet had a large, sickle-shaped claw on the second toe.

- **Because** it was a small dinosaur, *Deinonychus* would have fed on small mammals, juvenile dinosaurs, and lizards.

- **A pack of *Deinonychus*** hunting together could have brought down a large dinosaur, jumping on it and slashing it with their claws. The stiff tail would help it balance during such movements.

- **It has been suggested** that *Deinonycthus* was warm-blooded. Birds may have evolved from this type of dinosaur.

◀ *Packs of* Deinonychus *may have been able to outrun larger dinosaurs, bring them down, and kill them for food.*

Pterodactyls

- **Pterodactyls** belong to a group of flying reptiles called the pterosaurs.
- **Pterosaurs** lived during the Triassic, Jurassic, and Cretaceous periods, at the same time as the dinosaurs.
- **Pterodactyls** are found fossilized in rocks of Jurassic and Cretaceous age.
- **The first fossil** pterosaur was discovered in southern Germany in 1784.
- **At first** this fossil was thought to be of an aquatic creature. Later studies found it to be of extremely light construction, and its very long fourth finger was interpreted as a wing support.

▲ *Pterosaurs, like the* Pterodactylus, *could glide but could not fly as efficiently as most birds—their wings were far less flexible.*

186

- **The name** *Pterodactylus* (wing finger) was given to this German fossil.

- **The bones** of *Pterodactylus* were hollow to minimize the creature's weight—an adaptation for flight.

- *Pterodactylus* had a long beaklike snout and claws at the front corners of its leathery wings.

- **A detailed study** of the brain-cases of some pterodactyl skulls shows that these creatures had large brains, which were in some respects similar to those of birds.

- *Pterodactylus* probably flew in a gliding fashion, and may have swooped down to catch prey.

▼ Pteranodon *was one of the later and larger pterosaurs and lived about 70 million years ago. It swooped over the sea to scoop up fish. Its wingspan was up to 33 ft.*

Diplodocus

▶ *Diplodocus had large eyes, but a minute, egg-sized brain.*

- **Diplodocus** was a giant herbivore, and it lived at the end of the Jurassic Period, around 150 million years ago.

- **Weighing around** 10–20 tons, *Diplodocus* was one of the lighter large quadrupeds. It was, however, the longest of this type of dinosaur, being about 90 ft in length.

- **Diplodocid fossils** have been found in North America, especially in Colorado and Wyoming.

- **With a large body** to support, *Diplodocus* stood on four massive legs. These had hooflike claws, apart from the three inner toes, which had sharper, longer claws.

  - **The thick legs** acted like the supports on a suspension bridge, with its backbone in the same position as the roadway between them.

    - **The neck** and tail were very long. The tail tapered gradually, and had a whiplike end.

    - **A modern** interpretation of the animal's body suggests that the tail did not drag on the ground, as had been previously thought. It was almost certainly held well off the ground.

    - **The skull** of *Diplodocus* had large eye sockets, and nostrils positioned high above the jaws, which had thin teeth set right at the front. The brain-case was tiny, about the size of a hen's egg.

  - **Like other giant sauropods**, *Diplodocus* was a herbivore. The teeth did no more than tear off leaves. In the stomach these were broken up by gastroliths (swallowed stones).

...FASCINATING FACT...

Diplodocus's nostrils were so high up on its skull that experts once thought it had a trunk like an elephant's.

Footprints and dinosaur movement

- **As a dinosaur moved**, it left footprints in sand or mud, just as a modern animal does. If sediment washed into the footprint impression, a trace fossil could be formed.

- **Different footprints** can be made by the same dinosaur, depending on how wet the mud is, and how fast the animal is moving.

- **As well as** individual footprints being common in certain places, there are many famous dinosaur trackways.

- **Dinosaur** trackways are found at the Paluxy River in Texas, at Peace River Canyon in Canada, and in the UK at Swanage in Dorset and near Scarborough in North Yorkshire.

- **In Queensland**, Australia, there is evidence of a dinosaur stampede, with the tracks of over 130 different dinosaurs.

- **Both the size and speed** of a dinosaur can be calculated from its footprints.

- **By studying** modern animals and their movement, a formula has been worked out that relates to an animal's length of stride, body weight, and speed.

- **The trackway** at the Paluxy River in Texas shows adult sauropods moving at 2 mph and smaller ones, possibly the young, walking at 2.5 mph.

- **The dinosaur** stampede in Queensland, Australia, suggests dinosaurs running at 8–9 mph, and a giant carnivore walking at 5 mph.

◀ *These footprints were left by a* Tyrannosaurus. *The method of working out the animal's size, based on its footprints, can be backed up by evidence from fossil skeletons.*

Dinosaur eggs and nests

- **Fossils** of dinosaur eggs are not uncommon, proving that dinosaur young hatched from eggs with hard shells.

- **A hard-shelled egg** is a great evolutionary step forward from the soft eggs that amphibians and fish lay in water.

Hadrosaur egg

▶ *Both these dinosaur eggs are from late Cretaceous rocks in Henan Province, China.*

● **By laying** hard-shelled eggs, which were fertilized inside the mother, dinosaurs and birds no longer relied on a watery habitat.

● **Some scientists** believe that certain dinosaurs made nests of earth or mud and nested in colonies.

● **One of the earliest** discoveries of dinosaur nests was in the Gobi Desert in 1922.

● **It is difficult** to know how long a dinosaur egg took to hatch. It would depend on the surrounding temperature, and may have been many weeks.

Segnosaurus egg

● **Fossils** of *Protoceratops'* eggs show them laid in a circle, in a hollow scooped in the earth.

● *Maiasaura* was a hadrosaur (duck-billed dinosaur) found fossilized in late Cretaceous rocks in Montana.

● **From fossil evidence**, it seems that *Maiasaura* lived in large herds. They may have migrated seasonally and probably bred in colonies.

● **Fossils** of *Maiasaura* nests with eggs and young have been discovered in Montana.

Archaeopteryx

▼ *With a covering of feathers,* Archaeopteryx *is the earliest really birdlike creature in the fossil record.*

- **In 1861,** the fossil of an unknown creature that seemed to have the impressions of feathers was discovered at Solnhofen in southern Germany.

- **The fossils** from Solnhofen are called *Archaeopteryx*, which means "ancient wing."

- **This has proved** to be one of the most important fossils, as it is the earliest known bird.

- **The late Jurassic** limestone at Solnhofen is famous for its detailed preservation of very delicate organisms.

- *Archaeopteryx* has many features similar to those of small dinosaurs. Its jaws, for example, have rows of small teeth.

- **The reptilian tail** is also long and bony, and there are claws on its wing-supporting arms.

- **The presence of feathers**, and the large eyes and brain, are all true bird features.

- **The bones** in the *Archaeopteryx* skeleton are not as lightweight as those of modern birds.

- **It is probable** that *Archaeopteryx* could glide rather than fly efficiently.

▶ Archaeopteryx *feathers were proper flight feathers and were not just used for keeping warm.*

...FASCINATING FACT...

Only seven *Archaeopteryx* fossils have been found. Two had previously been cataloged as small dinosaurs.

The first mammals

- **Mammals** differ from reptiles in a number of important ways. They have fur, are warm-blooded, and feed their young with milk. Also, the great majority of mammals give birth to live young.

- **The first mammals** are found fossilized in rocks from the Triassic Period (248–206 million years ago).

- **Near Bristol, UK**, is a famous site for early mammal fossils. Here, deposits containing mammal remains from a Triassic cave floor were washed into a crack in the underlying Carboniferous limestone.

- **The early mammals** that lived at the same time as dinosaurs may have been at least partly nocturnal. Their skulls have large eye sockets, suggesting good vision.

- **In Jurassic rock** in South Africa are the remains of *Megazostrodon*, one of the best-documented early mammals.

- *Megazostrodon* had a shrewlike body and a long snout filled with sharp teeth.

- **It is thought that** *Megazostrodon* hunted at night for invertebrate prey, such as insects.

- **Another early mammal** was *Morganucodon*. This rodent-like creature had very large eye sockets in its tiny skull, and may also have been nocturnal.

- **The braincase** suggests good hearing as well as good vision. Paleontologists studying the jaws of *Morganucodon* believe that, like some modern mammals, it may have had two sets of teeth during its life, and was possibly fed on milk when very young.

▼ Megazostrodon *is one of the earliest*
mammals, and its fossils have been found
in rocks of Jurassic age.

Megatherium

- **After their development** through the Mesozoic Era, many giant forms of mammals evolved in the Cenozoic.

- **Tree sloths** evolved during the Eocene Epoch (56–34 million years ago).

- *Megatherium* was a close relation to the sloths and grew to more than 20 ft tall. It first appeared about six million years ago.

- **Fossil remains** of *Megatherium* have been found in both North and South America, mainly from cave deposits.

- **Much is known** about *Megatherium*, as it only became extinct around 12,000 years ago.

- **As well as bones**, some soft tissue and hair have been found.

- **There are stories** in Argentina that these giant sloths only died out a few hundred years ago, persecuted by humans.

- *Megatherium* had a thick tail and massive hind legs to support it when it stood upright.

- **The snout** was extended forward and it had no front teeth. The animal probably grasped tree branches with its strong front limbs and pulled off the leaves.

> **...FASCINATING FACT...**
> Large quantities of *Megatherium* dung are common in some caves in Argentina. One such deposit caught fire and burned for six months!

◀ Megatherium *used its considerable height to feed from trees. Few other mammals could compete with this feeding strategy.*

Paraceratherium

▶ Paraceratherium, *the largest land mammal ever, had strong legs and may have been able to run quite fast.*

- **Fossilized** remains of *Paraceratherium* (formerly known as either *Baluchitherium* or *Indricotherium*) have been found in Asia and Europe.

- *Paraceratherium* is classified as a perissodactyl.

- **These mammals** are characterized by having odd numbers of toes on their hoofs. Animals with hoofs are called ungulates.

- **Only about 19 or 20 species** of perissodactyls live today. Their even-toed ungulate cousins, the artiodactyls, have between 220–230 species living today.

- *Paraceratherium* lived during the Oligocene Epoch (34–23 million years ago).

- **This mammal** was a giant, hornless rhinoceros, with a long neck, and massive legs that supported its huge body.

- **The head** of *Paraceratherium* was relatively small, and, in the males, slightly dome-shaped.

- **Reaching** 18 ft in height at its shoulder, *Paraceratherium* was the largest known land mammal ever.

- **This enormous mammal** could easily reach the tops of quite tall trees to browse on leaves.

...FASCINATING FACT...

At 20 tons, *Paraceratherium* weighed as much as four large elephants. It may have lived in small groups like modern rhinoceroses.

Giant whales

▶ *The prehistoric whale* Basilosaurus, *which means "king of the lizards," was so named because the first person to examine its remains thought it was a gigantic plesiosaur—a prehistoric marine reptile.*

- **Mammals** took to the sea early during the Eocene Epoch, about 50 million years ago.

- **Most marine mammals** belong to the biological order Cetacea, which includes the whales, dolphins, and porpoises.

- **One of the oldest fossil whales**, *Pakicetus*, comes from Eocene rocks in Pakistan.

- **Fossils** of the giant Eocene whale, *Basilosaurus*, were first discovered in the 1830s.

- *Basilosaurus* grew to more than 65 ft in length. Its body was slim, and the head, with rows of large triangular teeth, was rather small. Modern whales have large heads.

- **Instead of** a blowhole like modern whales, *Basilosaurus* had nostrils.
- **The body** would have been able to flex in the water to provide power for swimming and the broad front flippers acted as rudders.
- **The rear limbs** were virtually nonexistent. They were simply small bony structures within the body.
- **In 1990**, new fossils of *Basilosaurus* were found, which showed that the insignificant internal rear limbs had all the bones of fully formed legs.
- **The largest** known animal to have ever lived, the modern blue whale, grows to 100 ft in length.

Ice Age monsters

- **The last** great Ice Age began around two million years ago. There have been some dramatic climate changes during this time.

- **Some mammals** grew to a great size during the Ice Age. Perhaps the best known is the wooly mammoth.

- **A fully grown** adult mammoth stood 9 ft tall at the shoulder.

- **The mammoth's skin** was well insulated, with a thick coat of hair.

- **One function** of the mammoth's huge tusks may have been to sweep snow away from the tundra vegetation on which it fed.

- **The remains** of mammoths have been found in Europe, Asia, and North America.

▲ *Wooly mammoths (1), musk ox (2), and giant elk (3) wander across the frozen tundra in search of vegetation to feed on.*

▲ *This mass of mammoth bones, including an almost complete set of ribs, is from Siberia, where it was found in frozen earth.*

- **Literally** tons of tusks and bones of wooly mammoths have been found.
- **Finds of mammoth tusks** have, in the past, been plundered for their ivory.
- **Our human ancestors** would have hunted mammoths for food. These elephants only became extinct about 10,000 years ago.

...FASCINATING FACT...
Mammoths fossilized in the tundra deep-freeze of Siberia
have flesh preserved well enough to be eaten.

Hominid fossils

- **Hominids** are mammals that belong to our "human" group. These creatures are different from apes and other primates because most probably walked upright on their hind legs.

- **There are many** different hominid fossils from various parts of the world, and it is not easy to work out a complete family tree.

- **The earliest** hominid fossils may be of a creature called *Ardipithecus* from Ethiopia.

- **An important group** of early hominids are the Australopithicenes. These upright-walking creatures lived in east and southern Africa between 3.5 million and two million years ago.

- **Working in Chad**, in central Africa, a team of French paleontologists found a hominid-like skull in 2002, which may be seven million years old. This may be a link between apes and hominids.

- **The earliest** fossils belonging to our genus, *Homo*, are the remains of *Homo habilis* from the world-famous Olduvai Gorge in Tanzania.

- **Many other species** of *Homo* have been discovered. Around two million years ago, *Homo ergaster* lived in Kenya.

- *Homo erectus* lived at the same time as *Homo ergaster* but in Europe and Asia. It became extinct only 50,000 years ago. *Homo erectus* could use fire.

- **Our own species** *Homo sapiens* began less than 200,000 years ago in Africa. Fossils trace its spread around the world.

- **Fossils** of *Homo neanderthalensis* have been found in many parts of Europe and Asia. These hominids were highly organized, and died out around 29,000 years ago.

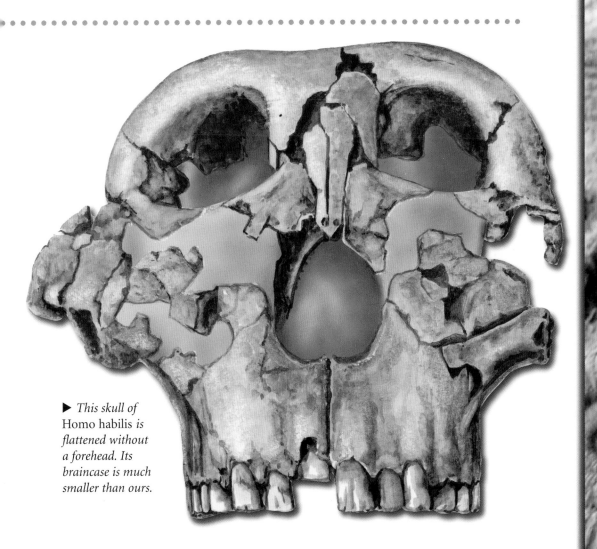

▶ *This skull of* Homo habilis *is flattened without a forehead. Its braincase is much smaller than ours.*

Glossary

Abyssal The deepest parts of the seabed, often thousands of miles from land.

Algae Simple, relatively primitive plants.

Calcite A common mineral composed of calcium carbonate. Calcite is found in shells and bones, and limestone is largely composed of this mineral.

Carapace exoskeleton The outer skeleton of an arthropod.

Chert A rock made almost completely of silicon dioxide. Chert often occurs as nodular masses in limestone strata. Flint is a form of chert.

Class A group of broadly similar organisms. A number of genera are grouped in a class. There are many classes within a phylum.

Compound eyes Eyes that have numerous lenses.

Continental shelf The relatively shallow part of the ocean. It extends from the shore to the continental slope, where the seabed falls to the abyssal plain.

Correlate To link strata from place to place, usually by using the fossils they contain.

Delta A deposit of sediment that accumulates where a river enters a body of nonflowing water, such as the sea or a lake.

Epoch A subdivision of geological time, shorter than a period.

Era A large part of geological time that can be divided into periods.

Genus A group of broadly similar species. Many genera make up a family, and many families make up a phylum.

Ice Age A period of time when worldwide temperatures are very low. This allows glaciers and ice sheets to develop and spread further away from the poles than today.

Igneous rocks Rocks formed when magma (molten rock below the ground) or lava (molten rock on the Earth's surface) harden into rock.

Invertebrate Creatures without an internal bony skeleton.

Metamorphism Changes that happen to existing rocks and are caused by heat or pressure, or a combination of both. Metamorphism usually occurs deep in the Earth's crust, though lava flowing on the surface can metamorphose rocks over which it flows.

Organism A living plant or animal.

Ooze Very fine-grained sediment that is found on the bed of the deepest seas.

Period A large part of geological time. Eras are subdivided into periods.

Phylum A large group of similar organisms. A phylum is divided up into families, genera, and species.

Plankton Tiny organisms that drift in the sea, often near the surface.

Quartz A very common mineral made of silicon dioxide. Sandstone is mainly made of small grains of this mineral.

Radiometric dating A way of obtaining absolute ages for rocks, based on the decay of radioactive minerals. It is mainly used for igneous and metamorphic rocks.

Reef An underwater bank of sediment or rock, the top of which is very near to sea level.

Sediment The sand, mud, and other loose material from which sedimentary rocks are formed.

Species A group of virtually identical organisms that can breed with each other.

Stratigraphy The science of placing rocks in the correct time sequence.

Strip mining Mining on the Earth's surface, not underground. Any material lying above the valuable rock or mineral being mined is stripped away. This is a type of open-cast mining.

Time scale The list of eras and periods, with their dates, that are used for subdividing geological time.

Xylem Plant tissue that carries fluids and supports the plant.

Index

Index

Index

Index

217

Index

Index

Index

Acknowledgments

The publishers would like to thank the following
artist whose work appears in this book:

Mike Saunders

All other artworks are from the Miles Kelly Artwork Bank

The publishers would like to thank the following picture
sources whose photographs appear in this book:

Page 22 Michael Siller/Fotolia.com
Page 121 Christian13/Fotolia.com
Page 125 Bradford Lumley/Fotolia.com
Page 173 Louie Psihoyos/CORBIS
Page 166 Johnathon Blair/CORBIS

All other photographs courtesy of
Chris and Helen Pellant